Dancing at Lughnasa

A play

Brian Friel

Samuel French - London
New York - Toronto - Hollywood

0573 017425 0223 6B

In memory of those five brave Glenties women

IMPORTANT NOTICE

The issue of a licence by Samuel French Ltd to perform *Dancing at Lughnasa* requires that in all instances in which the title of the play appears for the purpose of advertising, publicizing or otherwise exploiting the play and/or production (including, without limitation, programmes, souvenir booklets and playbills) the author's name must also appear, but on a separate line in which no other name appears, immediately following the title:

DANCING AT LUGHNASA
BRIAN FRIEL

Furthermore, the author's name must be in a size at least seventy-five per cent of the play's title, and no other person connected with the licensed production shall be given billing larger than fifty per cent of the play's title.

It is a condition of the licence issued that the original productions of *Dancing at Lughnasa* are credited as follows:

World première at the Abbey Theatre, Dublin
24th April 1990

British première at the Lyttelton Theatre
at the Royal National Theatre, London,
15th October 1990

Opened at the Phoenix Theatre, London
produced by Bill Kenwright and Noel Pearson
25th March 1991

Originally produced on the New York stage
by Noel Pearson in association with Bill Kenwright and Joseph Harris
opened at the Plymouth Theatre
24th October 1991

CHARACTERS

Michael, young man, narrator
Kate, forty, schoolteacher
Maggie, thirty-eight, housekeeper
Agnes, thirty-five, knitter
Rose, thirty-two, knitter
Chris, twenty-six, Michael's mother
Gerry, thirty-three, Michael's father
Jack, fifty-three, missionary priest

Michael, who narrates the story, also speaks the lines of the boy, i.e. himself when he was seven

The action takes place in the home of the Mundy family, two miles outside the village of Ballybeg, County Donegal, Ireland

ACT I   A warm day in early August
ACT II   Three weeks later

Time—1936

DANCING AT LUGHNASA

World première at the Abbey Theatre, Dublin on 24th
April 1990 with the following cast of characters:

Kate	Frances Tomelty
Maggie	Anita Reeves
Rose	Brid Ni Neachtain
Agnes	Brid Brennan
Chris	Catherine Byrne
Michael	Gerald McSorley
Gerry	Paul Herzberg
Jack	Barry McGovern

Director: Patrick Mason
Designer: Joe Vanek
Lighting: Trevor Dawson
Choreographer: Terry John Bates

The British première was at the Lyttelton Theatre at the
Royal National Theatre, London on 15th October 1990
with the following cast of characters:

Michael	Gerald McSorley
Chris	Catherine Byrne
Maggie	Anita Reeves
Agnes	Brid Brennan
Rose	Brid Ni Neachtain
Kate	Rosaleen Linehan
Gerry	Stephen Dillane
Jack	Alec McCowen

Director: Patrick Mason
Designer: Joe Vanek
Lighting: Trevor Dawson
Choreographer: Terry John Bates

The play, produced by Bill Kenwright and Noel Pearson, opened at the Phoenix Theatre, London on 25th March 1991 with the following cast:

Michael	Gerald McSorley
Kate	Rosaleen Linehan
Maggie	Anita Reeves
Agnes	Brid Brennan
Rose	Brid Ni Neachtain
Chris	Catherine Byrne
Gerry	Robert Gwilym
Jack	Alec McCowen

Director: Patrick Mason
Designer: Joe Vanek
Lighting: Trevor Dawson
Choreographer: Terry John Bates

The play was originally produced on the New York stage by Noel Pearson in association with Bill Kenwright and Joseph Harris at the Plymouth Theatre, New York on 24th October 1991 with the following cast of characters:

Michael	Gerald McSorley
Kate	Rosaleen Linehan
Maggie	Dearbhla Molloy
Agnes	Brid Brennan
Rose	Brid Ni Neachtain
Chris	Catherine Byrne
Gerry	Robert Gwilym
Jack	Donal Donnelly

Director: Patrick Mason
Designer: Joe Vanek
Lighting: Trevor Dawson
Choreographer: Terry John Bates

AUTHOR'S NOTE

Set

Slightly more than half the area of the stage is taken up by the kitchen R.
The rest of the stage—i.e. the remaining area L—is the garden adjoining the
house. The garden is neat but not cultivated.

UC is a garden seat.

The (unseen) boy has been making two kites in the garden and pieces of
wood, paper, cord, etc., are lying on the ground close to the garden seat.
One kite is almost complete.

There are two doors leading out of the kitchen. The front door leads to
the garden and the front of the house. The second in the top R corner leads
to the bedrooms and to the area behind the house.

One kitchen window looks out front. A second window looks on to the
garden.

There is a sycamore tree off R. One of its branches reaches over part of the
house.

The room has the furnishings of the usual country kitchen of the thirties:
a large iron range, large turf box beside it, table and chairs, dresser, oil lamp,
buckets with water at the back door, etc., etc. But because this is the home of
five women the austerity of the furnishings is relieved by some gracious
touches—flowers, pretty curtains, an attractive dresser arrangement, etc.

Dress

Kate, the teacher, is the only wage-earner. Agnes and Rose make a little
money knitting gloves at home. Chris and Maggie have no income. So the
clothes of all the sisters reflect their lean circumstances. Rose wears
wellingtons even though the day is warm. Maggie wears large boots with
long, untied laces. Rose, Maggie and Agnes all wear the drab, wrap-around
overalls/aprons of the time.

In the opening tableau Father Jack is wearing the uniform of a British
army officer chaplain—a magnificent and immaculate uniform of dazzling
white; gold epaulettes and gold buttons, tropical hat, clerical collar, military
cane. He stands stiffly to attention. As the text says he is "resplendent",
"magnificent". So resplendent that he looks almost comic opera.

In this tableau, too, Gerry is wearing a spotless white tricorn hat with
splendid white plumage. (Soiled and shabby versions of Jack's uniform and
Gerry's ceremonial hat are worn at the end of the play, i.e. in the final
tableau.)

Rose is "simple". All her sisters are kind to her and protective of her. But
Agnes has taken on the role of special protector.

ACT I

When the play opens Michael is standing DL *in a pool of light. The rest of the stage is in darkness. Immediately Michael begins speaking, slowly bring up the Lights on the rest of the stage*

Around the stage and at a distance from Michael the other characters stand motionless in formal tableau. Maggie is at the kitchen window R *Chris is at the front door. Kate at extreme* R. *Rose and Gerry sit on the garden seat. Jack stands beside Rose. Agnes is* UL. *They hold these positions while Michael talks to the audience*

Michael When I cast my mind back to that summer of 1936 different kinds of memories offer themselves to me. We got our first wireless set that summer—well, a sort of a set; and it obsessed us. And because it arrived as August was about to begin, my Aunt Maggie—she was the joker of the family—she suggested we give it a name. She wanted to call it Lugh* after the old Celtic God of the Harvest. Because in the old days August the First was *Lá Lughnasa*, the feast day of the pagan god, Lugh; and the days and weeks of harvesting that followed were called the Festival of Lughnasa. But Aunt Kate—she was a national schoolteacher and a very proper woman—she said it would be sinful to christen an inanimate object with any kind of name, not to talk of a pagan god. So we just called it Marconi because that was the name enblazoned on the set.

And about three weeks before we got that wireless, my mother's brother, my Uncle Jack, came home from Africa for the first time ever. For twenty-five years he had worked in a leper colony there, in a remote village called Ryanga in Uganda. The only time he ever left that village was for about six months during World War One when he was chaplain to the British army in East Africa. Then back to that grim hospice where he worked without a break for a further eighteen years. And now in his early fifties and in bad health he had come home to Ballybeg—as it turned out—to die.

And when I cast my mind back to that summer of 1936, these two memories—of our first wireless and of Father Jack's return—are always linked. So that when I recall my first shock at Jack's appearance, shrunken and jaundiced with malaria, at the same time I remember my first delight, indeed my awe, at the sheer magic of that radio. And when I remember the kitchen throbbing with the beat of Irish dance music beamed to us all the way from Dublin, and my mother and her sisters suddenly catching hands and dancing a spontaneous step-dance and

---

Lugh—pronounced "Loo". *Lughnasa*—pronounced "Lōō-na-sā".

laughing—screaming!—like excited schoolgirls, at the same time I see that forlorn figure of Father Jack shuffling from room to room as if he were searching for something but couldn't remember what. And even though I was only a child of seven at the time I know I had a sense of unease, some awareness of a widening breach between what seemed to be and what was, of things changing too quickly before my eyes, of becoming what they ought not to be. That may have been because Uncle Jack hadn't turned out at all like the resplendent figure in my head. Or maybe because I had witnessed Marconi's voodoo derange those kind, sensible women and transform them into shrieking strangers. Or maybe it was because during those Lughnasa weeks of 1936 we were visited on two occasions by my father, Gerry Evans, and for the first time in my life I had a chance to observe him.

The lighting changes. The kitchen and garden are now lit as for a warm summer afternoon

Michael, Kate, Gerry and Father Jack go off

The others busy themselves with their tasks. Maggie makes a mash for hens. Agnes knits gloves. Rose carries a basket of turf into the kitchen and empties it into the large box beside the range. Chris irons at the kitchen table. They all work in silence. Then Chris stops ironing, goes to the tiny mirror on the wall and scrutinizes her face

Chris When are we going to get a decent mirror to see ourselves in?
Maggie You can see enough to do you.
Chris I'm going to throw this aul cracked thing out.
Maggie Indeed you're not, Chrissie. I'm the one that broke it and the only way to avoid seven years bad luck is to keep on using it.
Chris You can see nothing in it.
Agnes Except more and more wrinkles.
Chris D'you know what I think I might do? I think I just might start wearing lipstick.
Agnes Do you hear this, Maggie?
Maggie Steady on, girl. Today it's lipstick; tomorrow it's the gin bottle.
Chris I think I just might.
Agnes As long as Kate's not around. "Do you want to make a pagan of yourself?"

Chris puts her face up close to the mirror and feels it

Chris Far too pale. And the aul mousey hair. Need a bit of colour.
Agnes What for?
Chris What indeed. (*She shrugs and goes back to her ironing. She holds up a surplice*) Make a nice dress that, wouldn't it? . . . God forgive me . . .

Work continues. Nobody speaks. Then suddenly and unexpectedly Rose bursts into raucous song

Rose   "Will you come to Abyssinia, will you come?
                Bring your own cup and saucer and a bun . . ."

(*As she sings the next two lines she dances—a gauche, graceless shuffle that defies the rhythm of the song*)

> "Mussolini will be there with his airplanes in the air,
> Will you come to Abyssinia, will you come?"

Not bad, Maggie—eh?

Maggie is trying to light a very short cigarette butt

Maggie You should be on the stage, Rose.

Rose continues to shuffle and now holds up her apron skirt

Rose And not a bad bit of leg, Maggie—eh?

Maggie Rose Mundy! Where's your modesty! (*She now hitches her own skirt even higher than Rose's and does a similar shuffle*) Is that not more like it?

Rose Good, Maggie—good—good! Look, Agnes, look!

Agnes A right pair of pagans, the two of you.

Rose Turn on Marconi, Chrissie.

Chris I've told you a dozen times: the battery's dead.

Rose It is not. It went for me a while ago. (*She goes to the set and switches it on. There is a sudden, loud three-second blast of "The British Grenadiers"*) You see! Takes aul Rosie! (*She is about to launch into a dance—and the music suddenly dies*)

Chris Told you.

Rose That aul set's useless.

Agnes Kate'll have a new battery back with her.

Chris If it's the battery that's wrong.

Rose Is Abyssinia in Africa, Aggie?

Agnes Yes.

Rose Is there a war there?

Agnes Yes. I've told you that.

Rose But that's not where Father Jack was, is it?

Agnes (*patiently*) Jack was in Uganda, Rosie. That's a different part of Africa. You know that.

Rose (*unhappily*) Yes, I do . . . I do . . . I know that . . .

Maggie catches her hand and sings softly into her ear to the same melody as the "Abyssinia" song

Maggie   "Will you vote for De Valera, will you vote?
         If you don't, we'll be like Gandhi with his goat."

Rose and Maggie now sing the next two lines together

Rose ⎫
Maggie ⎬ "Uncle Bill from Baltinglass has a wireless up his——
(*They dance as they sing the final line of the song*)
         Will you vote for De Valera, will you vote?"

Maggie I'll tell you something, Rosie: the pair of us should be on the stage.

Rose The pair of us should be on the stage, Aggie!

They return to their tasks. Agnes goes to the cupboard for wool. On her way back to her seat she looks out the window that looks on to the garden

Agnes What's that son of yours at out there?
Chris God knows. As long as he's quiet.
Agnes He's making something. Looks like a kite. (*She taps on the window; calling*) Michael! (*She blows a kiss to the imaginary child*) Oh, that was the wrong thing to do! He's going to have your hair, Chris.
Chris Mine's like a whin-bush. Will you wash it for me tonight, Maggie?
Maggie Are we all for a big dance somewhere?
Chris After I've put Michael to bed. What about then?
Maggie I'm your man.
Agnes (*at the window*) Pity there aren't some boys about to play with.
Maggie Now you're talking. Couldn't we all do with that?
Agnes (*leaving the window*) Maggie!
Maggie Wouldn't it be just great if we had a . . . (*She breaks off*) Shhh.
Chris What is it?
Maggie Thought I heard Father Jack at the back door. I hope Kate remembers his quinine.
Agnes She'll remember. Kate forgets nothing.

Pause

Rose There's going to be pictures in the hall next Saturday, Aggie. I think maybe I'll go.
Agnes (*guarded*) Yes?
Rose I might be meeting somebody there.
Agnes Who's that?
Rose I'm not saying.
Chris Do we know him?
Rose I'm not saying.
Agnes You'll enjoy that, Rosie. You loved the last picture we saw.
Rose And he wants to bring me up to the back hills next Sunday—up to Lough Anna. His father has a boat there. And I'm thinking maybe I'll bring a bottle of milk with me. And I've enough money saved to buy a packet of chocolate biscuits.
Chris Danny Bradley is a scut, Rose.
Rose I never said it was Danny Bradley!
Chris He's a married man with three young children.
Rose And that's just where you're wrong, missy—so there! (*To Agnes*) She left him six months ago, Aggie, and went to England.
Maggie Rose, love, we just want——
Rose (*to Chris*) And who are you to talk, Christina Mundy! Don't you dare lecture me!
Maggie Everybody in the town knows that Danny Bradley is——
Rose (*to Maggie*) And you're jealous, too! That's what's wrong with the whole of you—you're jealous of me! (*To Agnes*) He calls me his Rosebud. He waited for me outside the chapel gate last Christmas morning and he gave me this. (*She opens the front of her apron. A charm and a medal are pinned to her jumper*) "That's for my Rosebud," he said.
Agnes Is it a fish, Rosie?
Rose Isn't it lovely? It's made of pure silver. And it brings you good luck.

Agnes It is lovely.
Rose I wear it all the time—beside my miraculous medal. (*Pause*) I love him, Aggie.
Agnes I know.
Chris (*softly*) Bastard.

Rose closes the front of her apron. She is on the point of tears. Silence. Now Maggie lifts her hen-bucket and using it as a dancing partner she does a very fast and very exaggerated tango across the kitchen floor as she sings in her parodic style the words from "The Isle of Capri"

Maggie   "Summer time was nearly over;
                    Blue Italian skies above.
                    I said, 'Mister, I'm a rover.
                    Can't you spare a sweet word of love?' "

(*And without pausing for breath she begins calling her hens as she exits by the back door*) Tchook-tchook-tchook-tchook-tchook-tchook-tchook-tchookeeeeeee . . .

Maggie goes

Michael enters and stands L

Rose takes the lid off the range and throws turf into the fire

Chris For God's sake, I have an iron in there!
Rose How was I to know that?
Chris Don't you see me ironing? (*Fishing with the tongs*) Now you've lost it. Get out of my road, will you!
Agnes Rosie, love, would you give me a hand with this (*of wool*). If we don't work a bit faster we'll never get two dozen pairs finished this week.

The convention must now be established that the (imaginary) Boy Michael is working at the kite materials lying on the ground. No dialogue with the Boy Michael must ever be addressed directly to adult Michael, the narrator. Here, for example, Maggie has her back to the narrator. Michael responds to Maggie in his ordinary narrator's voice

Maggie enters the garden from the back of the house

Maggie What are these supposed to be?
Boy Kites.
Maggie Kites! God help your wit!
Boy Watch where you're walking, Aunt Maggie—you're standing on a tail.
Maggie Did it squeal?—haaaa! I'll make a deal with you, cub: I'll give you a penny if those things ever leave the ground. Right?
Boy You're on.
Maggie (*now squatting down beside him*) I've new riddles for you.
Boy Give up.
Maggie What goes round the house and round the house and sits in the corner? (*Pause*) A broom! Why is a river like a watch?
Boy You're pathetic.

Maggie Because it never goes far without winding! Hairy out and hairy in, lift your foot and stab it in—what is it?

Pause

Boy Give up.
Maggie Think!
Boy Give up.
Maggie Have you even one brain in your head?
Boy Give up.
Maggie A sock!
Boy A what?
Maggie A sock—a sock! You know—lift your foot and stab it—

She demonstrates. No response

D'you know what your trouble is, cub? You-are-buck-stupid!
Boy Look out—there's a rat!

She screams and leaps to her feet in terror

Maggie Where—where—where—Jesus, Mary and Joseph, where is it?
Boy Caught you again, Aunt Maggie.
Maggie You evil wee brat—God forgive you! I'll get you for that, Michael! Don't you worry—I won't forget that! (*She picks up her bucket and moves off towards the back of the house. Stops*) And I had a barley sugar sweet for you.
Boy Are there bits of cigarette tobacco stuck to it?
Maggie Jesus Christ! Some day you're going to fill some woman's life with happiness. (*Moving off*) Tchook-tchook-tchook-tchook ... (*Again she stops and throws him a sweet*) There. I hope it chokes you. (*She goes*) Tchook-tchook-tchook-tchook-tchookeeeee ...

Maggie exits

Michael When I saw Uncle Jack for the first time the reason I was so shocked by his appearance was that I expected—well, I suppose, the hero from a schoolboy's book. Once I had seen a photograph of him radiant and splendid in his officer's uniform. It had fallen out of Aunt Kate's prayer book and she snatched it from me before I could study it in detail. It was a picture taken in 1917 when he was a chaplain to the British forces in East Africa and he looked—magnificent. But Aunt Kate had been involved locally in the War of Independence; so Father Jack's brief career in the British army was never referred to in that house. All the same the wonderful Father Jack of that photo was the image of him that lodged in my mind.

But if he was a hero to me, he was a hero and a saint to my mother and to my aunts. They pored over his occasional letters. They prayed every night for him and for his lepers and for the success of his mission. They scraped and saved for him—sixpence here, a shilling there—sacrifices they made willingly, joyously, so that they would have a little money to send to him at Christmas and for his birthday. And every so often when a story would appear in the *Donegal Enquirer* about "our own leper priest", as they called him—because Ballybeg was proud of him, the whole of Donegal was proud of him—it was only natural that our family would enjoy a small share of that fame—it gave us that little bit of status in the eyes of the parish. And it must have helped my aunts to bear the shame Mother brought on the household by having me—as it was called then— out of wedlock.

Kate enters L, *laden with shopping bags*

When she sees the boy working at his kites her face lights up with pleasure. She watches him for a few seconds. Then she goes to him

Kate Well, that's what I call a busy man. Come here and give your Aunt Kate a big kiss. (*She catches his head between her hands and kisses the crown of his head*) And what's all this? It's a kite, is it? (*She kneels beside him*)

Boy It's two kites.

Kate (*inspecting them*) It certainly is two kites. And they're the most wonderful kites I've ever seen. And what are these designs? (*She studies the kite faces which the audience cannot see*)

Boy They're faces. I painted them.

Kate (*pretended horror*) Oh, good Lord, they put the heart across me! You did those? Oh, God bless us, those are scarifying! What are they? Devils? Ghosts? I wouldn't like to see those lads up in the sky looking down at me! Hold on now ... (*She searches in her bags and produces a small wooden spinning-top and whip*) Do you know what this is? Of course you do—a spinning-top. Good boy. And this—this is the whip. You know how to use it? Indeed you do. What do you say?

Boy Thanks.

Kate Thank you, Aunt Kate. And do you know what I have in here? A new library book! With coloured pictures! We'll begin reading it at bedtime. (*Again she kisses the top of his head. She gets to her feet*) Call me the moment you're ready to fly them. I wouldn't miss that for all the world. (*She goes into the kitchen*) D'you know what he's at out there? Did you see, Christina? Making two kites!

Chris Some kites he'll make.

Kate All by himself. No help from anybody.

Agnes You always said he was talented, Kate.

Kate No question about that. And very mature for his years.

Chris Very cheeky for his years.

Rose I think he's beautiful, Chris. I wish he was mine.

Chris Is that a spinning-top he has?

Kate It's nothing.

Michael exits L

Chris Oh, Kate, you have him spoiled. Where did you get it?

Kate Morgan's Arcade.

Chris And I'm sure he didn't even thank you.

Rose I know why you went into Morgan's!

Kate He did indeed. He's very mannerly.
Rose You wanted to see Austin Morgan!
Kate Every field along the road—they're all out at the hay and the corn.
Rose Because you have a notion of that aul Austin Morgan!
Kate Going to be a good harvest by the look of it.
Rose I know you have! She's blushing! Look! Isn't she blushing?

Chris holds up a skirt she is ironing

Chris You'd need to put a stitch in that hem, Rosie.
Rose (*to Kate*) But what you don't know is that he's going with a wee young thing from Carrickfad.
Kate Rose, what Austin Morgan does or doesn't do with——
Rose Why are you blushing then? She's blushing, isn't she? Why-why-why, Kate?
Kate (*sudden anger*) For God's sake, Rose, shut up, would you!
Rose Anyhow we all know you always had a——
Agnes Rosie, pass me those steel needles—would you, please?

Pause

Chris (*to Kate*) Are you tired?

Kate flops into a seat

Kate That road from the town gets longer every day. You can laugh if you want but I *am* going to get that old bike fixed up and I *am* going to learn to ride this winter.
Agnes Many about Ballybeg?
Kate Ballybeg's off its head. I'm telling you. Everywhere you go—everyone you meet—it's the one topic: Are you going to the harvest dance? Who are you going with? What are you wearing? This year's going to be the biggest ever and the best ever.
Agnes All the same I remember some great harvest dances.
Chris Don't we all.
Kate (*unpacking*) Another of those riveting Annie M. P. Smithson novels for you, Agnes.
Agnes Ah. Thanks.
Kate *The Marriage of Nurse Harding*—oh, dear! For you, Christina. One teaspoonful every morning before breakfast.
Chris What's this?
Kate Cod-liver oil. You're far too pale.
Chris Thank you, Kate.
Kate Because you take no exercise. Anyhow I'm in the chemist's shop and this young girl—a wee slip of a thing, can't even remember her name—her mother's the knitting agent that buys your gloves, Agnes——
Agnes Vera McLaughlin.
Kate Her daughter whatever you call her.
Rose Sophia.
Kate Miss Sophia, who must be all of fifteen; she comes up to me and she says, "I hope you're not going to miss the harvest dance, Miss Mundy. It's going to be just *supreme* this year." And honest to God, if you'd seen

the delight in her eyes, you'd think it was heaven she was talking about. I'm telling you—off its head—like a fever in the place. That's the quinine. The doctor says it won't cure the malaria but it might help to contain it. Is he in his room?

Chris He's wandering about out the back somewhere.

Kate I told the doctor you thought him very quiet, Agnes.

Agnes has stopped knitting and is looking abstractedly into the middle distance

Agnes Yes?

Kate Well, didn't you? And the doctor says we must remember how strange everything here must be to him after so long. And on top of that Swahili has been his language for twenty-five years; so that it's not his mind is confused—it's just that he has difficulty finding the English words for what he wants to say.

Chris No matter what the doctor says, Kate, his mind is a bit confused. Sometimes he doesn't know the difference between us. I've heard him calling you Rose and he keeps calling me some strange name like——

Kate Okawa.

Chris That's it! Aggie, you've heard him, haven't you?

Kate Okawa was his house boy. He was very attached to him. (*Taking off her shoe*) I think I'm getting corns in this foot. I hope to God I don't end up crippled like poor Mother, may she rest in peace.

Agnes Wouldn't it be a good one if we all went?

Chris Went where?

Agnes To the harvest dance.

Chris Aggie!

Agnes Just like we used to. All dressed up. I think I'd go.

Rose I'd go, too, Aggie! I'd go with you!

Kate For heaven's sake you're not serious, Agnes—are you?

Agnes I think I am.

Kate Hah! There's more than Ballybeg off its head.

Agnes I think we should all go.

Kate Have you any idea what it'll be like?—Crawling with checky young brats that I taught years ago.

Agnes I'm game.

Chris We couldn't, Aggie—could we?

Kate And all the riff-raff of the countryside.

Agnes I'm game.

Chris Oh God, you know how I loved dancing, Aggie.

Agnes (*to Kate*) What do you say?

Kate (*to Chris*) You have a seven-year-old child—have you forgotten that?

Agnes (*to Chris*) You could wear that blue dress of mine—you have the figure for it and it brings out the colour of your eyes.

Chris Can I have it? God, Aggie, I could dance non-stop all night—all week—all month!

Kate And who'd look after Father Jack?

Agnes (*to Kate*) And you look great in that cotton dress you got for confirmation last year. You're beautiful in it, Kate.

Kate What sort of silly talk is——

Agnes (*to Kate*) And you can wear my brown shoes with the crossover straps.
Kate This is silly talk. We can't, Agnes. How can we?
Rose Will Maggie go with us?
Chris Will Maggie what! Try to stop her!
Kate Oh God, Agnes, what do you think?
Agnes We're going.
Kate Are we?
Rose We're off! We're away!
Kate Maybe we're mad—are we mad?
Chris It costs four and six to get in.
Agnes I've five pounds saved. I'll take you. I'll take us all.
Kate Hold on now——
Agnes How many years has it been since we were at the harvest dance?—at any dance? And I don't care how young they are, how drunk and dirty and sweaty they are. I want to dance, Kate. It's the Festival of Lughnasa. I'm only thirty-five. I want to dance.
Kate (*wretched*) I know, I know, Agnes, I know. All the same—oh my God—I don't know if it's——
Agnes It's settled. We're going—the Mundy girls—all five of us together.
Chris Like we used to.
Agnes Like we used to.
Rose I love you, Aggie! I love you more than chocolate biscuits!

Rose kisses Agnes impetuously, flings her arms above her head, begins singing "Abyssinia" and does the first steps of a bizarre and abandoned dance. At this Kate panics

Kate No, no, no! We're going nowhere!
Chris If we all want to go——
Kate Look at yourselves, will you! Just look at yourselves! Dancing at our time of day? That's for young people with no duties and no responsibilities and nothing in their heads but pleasure.
Agnes Kate, I think we——
Kate Do you want the whole countryside to be laughing at us?—women of our years?—mature women, *dancing*? What's come over you all? And this is Father Jack's home—we must never forget that—ever. No, no, we're going to no harvest dance.
Rose But you just said——
Kate And there'll be no more discussion about it. The matter's over. I don't want it mentioned again.

Silence

Michael enters L. Maggie returns to the garden from the back of the house. She has the hen bucket on her arm and her hands are cupped as if she were holding something fragile between them. She goes to the kite materials

Maggie The fox is back.
Boy Did you see him?
Maggie He has a hole chewed in the henhouse door.

Boy Did you get a look at him, Aunt Maggie?
Maggie Wasn't I talking to him. He was asking for you.
Boy Ha-ha. What's that you have in your hands?
Maggie Something I found.
Boy What?
Maggie Sitting very still at the foot of the holly tree.
Boy Show me.
Maggie Say please three times.
Boy Please-please-please.
Maggie In Swahili.
Boy Are you going to show it to me or are you not?
Maggie (*crouching down beside him*) Now, cub, put your ear over here. Listen. Shhh. D'you hear it?
Boy I think so . . . yes.
Maggie What do you hear?
Boy Something.
Maggie Are you sure?
Boy Yes, I'm sure. Show me, Aunt Maggie.
Maggie All right. Ready? Get back a bit. Bit further. Right?
Boy Yes.

Suddenly she opens her hands and her eyes follow the rapid and imaginary flight of something up to the sky and out of sight. She continues staring after it. Pause

What was it?
Maggie Did you see it?
Boy I think so . . . yes.
Maggie Wasn't it wonderful?
Boy Was it a bird?
Maggie The colours are so beautiful. (*She gets to her feet*) Trouble is—just one quick glimpse— that's all you ever get. And if you miss that . . . (*She moves off towards the back door of the kitchen*)
Boy What was it, Aunt Maggie?
Maggie Don't you know what it was? It was all in your mind. Now we're quits.

Michael exits during the following

Kate (*unpacking*) Tea . . . soap . . . Indian meal . . . jelly . . .
Maggie I'm sick of that white rooster of yours, Rosie. Some pet that. Look at the lump he took out of my arm.
Rose You don't speak to him right.
Maggie I know the speaking he'll get from me—the weight of my boot. Would you put some turf on that fire, Chrissie; I'm going to make some soda bread. (*She washes her hands and begins baking*)
Rose (*privately*) Watch out. She's in one of her cranky moods.
Kate Your ten Wild Woodbine, Maggie.
Maggie Great. The tongue's out a mile.
Rose (*privately*) You missed it all, Maggie.

Maggie What did I miss this time?
Rose We were all going to go to the harvest dance—like the old days. And
then Kate——
Kate Your shoes, Rose. The shoemaker says, whatever kind of feet you
have, only the insides of the soles wear down.
Rose Is that a bad thing?
Kate That is neither a bad thing nor a good thing, Rose. It's just—
distinctive, as might be expected.

Rose grimaces behind Kate's back

Cornflour . . . salt . . . tapioca—it's gone up a penny for some reason . . .
sugar for the bilberry jam—if we ever get the bilberries . . .

Agnes and Rose exchange looks

Maggie (*privately to Rose*) Look at the packet of Wild Woodbine she got
me.
Rose What's wrong with it?
Maggie Only nine cigarettes in it. They're so wild one of them must have
escaped on her.

They laugh secretly

Chris Doesn't Jack sometimes call you Okawa, too, Maggie?
Maggie Yes. What does it mean?
Chris Okawa was his house boy, Kate says.
Maggie Dammit. I thought it was Swahili for gorgeous.
Agnes Maggie!
Maggie That's the very thing we could do with here—a house boy.
Kate And the battery. The man in the shop says we go through these things
quicker than anyone in Ballybeg.
Chris Good for us. (*She takes the battery and leaves it beside Marconi*)
Kate I met the parish priest. I don't know what has happened to that man.
But ever since Father Jack came home he can hardly look me in the eye.
Maggie That's because you keep winking at him, Kate.
Chris He was always moody, that man.
Kate Maybe that's it . . . The paper . . . candles . . . matches . . . The word's
not good on that young Sweeney boy from the back hills. He was
anointed last night.
Maggie I didn't know he was dying?
Kate Not an inch of his body that isn't burned.
Agnes Does anybody know what happened?
Kate Some silly prank up in the hills. He knows he's dying, the poor boy.
Just lies there, moaning.
Chris What sort of prank?
Kate How would I know?
Chris What are they saying in the town?
Kate I know no more than I've told you, Christina.

Pause

Rose (*quietly, resolutely*) It was last Sunday week, the first night of the

Festival of Lughnasa; and they were doing what they do every year up there in the back hills.

Kate Festival of Lughnasa! What sort of——

Rose First they light a bonfire beside a spring well. Then they dance round it. Then they drive their cattle through the flames to banish the devil out of them.

Kate Banish the . . . ! You don't know the first thing about what——

Rose And this year there was an extra big crowd of boys and girls. And they were off their heads with drink. And young Sweeney's trousers caught fire and he went up like a torch. That's what happened.

Kate Who filled your head with that nonsense?

Rose They do it every Lughnasa. I'm telling you. That's what happened.

Kate (*very angry, almost shouting*) And they're savages! I know those people from the back hills! I've taught them! Savages—that's what they are! And what pagan practices they have are no concern of ours—none whatever! It's a sorry day to hear talk like that in a Christian home, a Catholic home! All I can say is that I'm shocked and disappointed to hear you repeating rubbish like that, Rose!

Rose (*quietly, resolutely*) That's what happened. I'm telling you.

Pause

Maggie All the same it would be very handy in the winter time to have a wee house boy to feed the hens: "Tchook-tchook-tchook-tchook-tchook-tchook tchook-tchookeeee . . ."

Father Jack enters by the back door. He looks frail and older than his fifty-three years. Broad-brimmed black hat. Heavy grey top coat. Woollen trousers that stop well short of his ankles. Heavy black boots. Thick woollen socks. No clerical collar. He walks—shuffles quickly—with his hands behind his back. He seems uneasy, confused. Scarcely any trace of an Irish accent

Jack I beg your pardon . . . the wrong apartment . . . forgive me . . .

Kate Come in and join us, Jack.

Jack May I?

Maggie You're looking well, Jack.

Jack Yes? I expected to enter my bedroom through that . . . what I am missing—what I require . . . I had a handkerchief in my pocket and I think perhaps I——

Chris (*taking one from the ironing pile*) Here's a handkerchief.

Jack I thank you. I am grateful. It is so strange: I don't remember the—the architecture?—the planning? what's the word?—the lay-out!— I don't recollect the lay-out of this home . . . scarcely. That is strange, isn't it? I thought the front door was there. (*To Kate*) You walked to the village to buy stores, Agnes?

Kate It's Kate. And dozens of people were asking for you.

Jack They remember me?

Kate Of course they remember you! And when you're feeling stronger they're going to have a great public welcome for you—flags, bands, speeches, everything!

Jack Why would they do this?

Kate Because they're delighted you're back.
Jack Yes?
Kate Because they're delighted you're home.
Jack I'm afraid I don't remember them. I couldn't name ten people in
Ballybeg now.
Chris It will all come back to you. Don't worry.
Jack You think so?
Agnes Yes, it will.
Jack Perhaps . . . I feel the climate so cold . . . if you'll forgive me . . .
Agnes Why don't you lie down for a while?
Jack May I do that . . . thank you . . . you are most kind . . .

He shuffles off

Pause. A sense of unease, almost embarrassment

Kate (_briskly_) It will be a slow process but he'll be fine. Apples . . . butter . . .
margarine . . . flour . . . And wait till you hear! Who did I meet in the post
office! Maggie, are you listening to me?
Maggie Yes?
Kate You'll never believe it—your old pal, Bernie O'Donnell! Home from
London! First time back in twenty years!
Maggie Bernie . . .
Kate Absolutely gorgeous. The figure of a girl of eighteen. Dressed to kill
from head to foot. And the hair!—as black and as curly as the day she left.
I can't tell you—a film star!
Maggie Bernie O'Donnell . . .
Kate And beside her two of the most beautiful children you ever laid eyes
on. Twins. They'll be fourteen next month. And to see the three of them
together—like sisters, I'm telling you.
Maggie Twin girls.
Kate Identical.
Maggie Identical.
Kate Nora and Nina.
Rose Mother used to say twins are a double blessing.
Maggie Bernie O'Donnell . . . oh my goodness . . .
Kate And wait till you hear—they're pure blond! "Where in the name of
God did the blond hair come from?" I asked her. "The father. Eric," she
says. "He's from Stockholm."
Agnes Stockholm!
Rose Where's Stockholm, Aggie?
Kate So there you are. Bernie O'Donnell married to a Swede. I couldn't
believe my eyes. But the same bubbly, laughing, happy Bernie. Asking
about everybody by name.

_Maggie goes to the window and looks out so that the others cannot see her
face. She holds her hands, covered with flour, out from her body_

Chris She remembered us all?
Kate Knew all about Michael; had his age to the very month. Was Agnes

still the quickest knitter in Ballybeg? Were none of us thinking of getting married?—and weren't we wise!

Rose Did she remember me?

Kate "Rose had the sweetest smile I ever saw."

Rose There!

Kate But asking specially for you, Maggie: how you were doing—what you were doing—how were you looking—were you as light-hearted as ever? Everytime she thinks of you, she says, she has the memory of the two of you hiding behind the turf stack, passing a cigarette between you and falling about laughing about some boy called—what was it?—Curley somebody?

Maggie Curley McDaid. An eejit of a fella. Bald as an egg at seventeen. Bernie O'Donnell . . . oh my goodness . . .

Pause

Agnes Will she be around for a while?

Kate Leaving tomorrow.

Agnes We won't see her so. That's a pity.

Chris Nice names, aren't they?—Nina and Nora.

Kate I like Nora. Nice name. Strong name.

Agnes Not so sure about Nina. (*To Chris*) Do you like Nina for a name?

Chris Nina? No, not a lot.

Kate Well, if there's a Saint Nina, I'm afraid she's not in my prayer book.

Agnes Maybe she's a Swedish saint.

Kate Saints in Sweden! What'll it be next!

Rose Mother used to say twins are a double blessing.

Kate (*sharply*) You've offered us that cheap wisdom already, Rose.

Pause

Chris You've got some flour on your nose, Maggie.

Maggie When I was sixteen I remember slipping out one Sunday night—it was this time of year, the beginning of August and Bernie and I met at the gate of the workhouse and the pair of us off to a dance in Ardstraw. I was being pestered by a fellow called Tim Carlin at the time but it was really Brian McGuinness that I was that I was keen on. Remember Brian with the white hands and the longest eyelashes you ever saw? But of course he was crazy about Bernie. Anyhow the two boys took us on the bar of their bikes and off the four of us headed to Ardstraw, fifteen miles each way. If Daddy had known, may he rest in peace . . .

And at the end of the night there was a competition for the Best Military Two-step. And it was down to three couples: the local pair from Ardstraw; wee Timmy and myself—he was up to there on me; and Brian and Bernie . . .

And they were just so beautiful together, so stylish; you couldn't take your eyes off them. People just stopped dancing and gazed at them . . .

And when the judges announced the winners—they were probably blind drunk—naturally the local couple came first; and Timmy and myself came second; and Brian and Bernie came third.

Poor Bernie was stunned. She couldn't believe it. Couldn't talk.
Wouldn't speak to any of us for the rest of the night. Wouldn't cycle
home with us. She was right, too: they should have won; they were just so
beautiful together ...
     And that's the last time I saw Brian McGuinness—remember Brian
with the ...? And the next thing I heard he had left for Australia ...
     She was right to be angry, Bernie. I know it wasn't fair—it wasn't fair
at all. I mean they must have been blind drunk, those judges, whoever
they were ...

*Maggie stands motionless, staring out of the window, seeing nothing. The
others drift back to their tasks: Rose and Agnes knit; Kate puts the groceries
away; Chris connects the battery. Pause*

Kate Is it working now, Christina?
Chris What's that?
Kate Marconi.
Chris Marconi? Yes, yes ... should be ...

*She switches the set on and returns to her ironing. The music, at first scarcely
audible, is Irish dance music—"The Mason's Apron", played by a ceili band.
Very fast; very heavy beat; a raucous sound. At first we are aware of the beat
only. Then, as the volume increases slowly, we hear the melody. For about ten
seconds—until the sound has established itself—the women continue with their
tasks. Then Maggie turns round. Her head is cocked to the beat, to the music.
She is breathing deeply, rapidly. Now her features become animated by a look
of defiance, of aggression; a crude mask of happiness. For a few seconds she
stands still, listening, absorbing the rhythm, surveying her sisters with her
defiant grimace. Now she spreads her fingers (which are covered with flour),
pushes her hair back from her face, pulls her hands down her cheeks and
patterns her face with an instant mask. At the same time she opens her mouth
and emits a wild, raucous "Yaaaah!"—and immediately begins to dance, arms,
legs, hair, long bootlaces flying. And as she dances she lilts—sings—shouts and
calls, "Come on and join me! Come on! Come on!" For about ten seconds she
dances alone—a white-faced, frantic dervish. Her sisters watch her*

*Then Rose's face lights up. Suddenly she flings away her knitting, leaps to her
feet, shouts, grabs Maggie's hand. They dance and sing—shout together;
Rose's wellington boots pounding out their own erratic rhythm. Now, after
another five seconds, Agnes looks around, leaps up, joins Maggie and Rose. Of
all the sisters she moves most gracefully, most sensuously. Then after the same
interval Chris, who has been folding Jack's surplice, tosses it quickly over her
head and joins in the dance. The moment she tosses the vestment over her head
Kate cries out in remonstration, "Oh, Christina—!" But her protest is
drowned. Agnes and Rose, Chris and Maggie, are now all doing a dance that is
almost recognizable. They meet—they retreat. They form a circle and wheel
round and round. But the movements seem caricatured; and the sound is too
loud; and the beat is too fast; and the almost recognizable dance is made
grotesque because—for example—instead of holding hands, they have their
arms tightly around one another's neck, one another's waist. Finally Kate, who*

has been watching the scene with unease, with alarm, suddenly leaps to her feet, flings her head back, and emits a loud "Yaaaah!"

Kate dances alone, totally concentrated, totally private; a movement that is simultaneously controlled and frantic; a weave of complex steps that takes her quickly round the kitchen, past her sisters, out to the garden, round the summer seat, back to the kitchen; a pattern of action that is out of character and at the same time ominous of some deep and true emotion. Throughout the dance Rose, Agnes, Maggie and Chris shout—call—sing to each other. Kate makes no sound

With this too loud music, this pounding beat, this shouting—calling—singing, this parodic reel, there is a sense of order being consciously subverted, of the women consciously and crudely caricaturing themselves, indeed of near-hysteria being induced. The music stops abruptly in mid-phrase. But because of the noise they are making the sisters do not notice and continue dancing for a few seconds. Then Kate notices—and stops. Then Agnes. Then Chris and Maggie. Now only Rose is dancing her graceless dance by herself. Then finally she, too, notices and stops. Silence. For some time they stand where they have stopped. There is no sound but their gasping for breath and short bursts of static from the radio. They look at each other obliquely; avoid looking at each other; half-smile in embarrassment; feel and look slightly ashamed and slightly defiant. Chris moves first. She goes to the radio

It's away again, that aul thing. Sometimes you're good with it, Aggie.
Agnes Feel the top. Is it warm?
Chris Roasting.
Agnes Turn it off till it cools down.

Chris turns it off—and slaps it

Chris Bloody useless set, that.
Kate No need for corner-boy language, Christina.
Agnes There must be some reason why it overheats.
Chris Because it's a goddamn, bloody useless set—that's why.
Rose Goddamn bloody useless.
Kate Are wellingtons absolutely necessary on a day like this, Rose?
Rose I've only my wellingtons and my Sunday shoes, Kate. And it's not Sunday, is it?
Kate Oh, dear, we're suddenly very logical, aren't we?
Maggie (*lighting a cigarette*) I'll tell you something, girls: this Ginger Rogers has seen better days.
Kate It's those cigarettes are killing you.
Maggie (*exhaling*) Wonderful Wild Woodbine. Next best thing to a wonderful, wild man. Want a drag, Kitty?
Kate Go and wash your face, Maggie. And for goodness' sake tie those laces.
Maggie Yes, miss. (*At the window*) Where's Michael, Chrissie?
Chris Working at those kites, isn't he?
Maggie He's not there. He's gone.
Chris He won't go far.

Maggie He was there ten minutes ago.
Chris He'll be all right.
Maggie But if he goes down to the old well——
Chris Just leave him alone for once, will you, please?

Maggie shrugs and goes out the back door

Pause

Kate Who's making the tea this evening?
Agnes Who makes the tea every evening?
Chris (*at the radio*) The connections seem to be all right.
Kate Please take that surplice off, Christina.
Chris Maybe a valve has gone—if I knew what a valve looked like.
Kate Have you no sense of propriety?
Chris If you ask me we should throw it out.
Agnes I'd be all for that. It's junk, that set.
Rose Goddamn and bloody useless.
Kate (*to Agnes*) And you'll buy a new one, will you?
Agnes It was never any good.
Kate You'll buy it out of your glove money, will you? I thought what you
  and Rose earned knitting gloves was barely sufficient to clothe the pair of
  you.
Agnes This isn't your classroom, Kate.
Kate Because I certainly don't see any of it being offered for the upkeep of
  the house.
Agnes Please, Kate——
Kate But now it stretches to buying a new wireless. Wonderful!
Agnes I make every meal you sit down to every day of the week——
Kate Maybe I should start knitting gloves?
Agnes I wash every stitch of clothes you wear. I polish your shoes. I make
  your bed. We both do—Rose and I. Paint the house. Sweep the chimney.
  Cut the grass. Save the turf. What you have here, Kate, are two unpaid
  servants.
Rose And d'you know what your nickname at school is? The Gander!
  Everybody calls you the Gander!

Maggie runs on and goes straight to the window

Maggie Come here till you see! Look who's coming up the lane!
Agnes Who's coming?
Maggie I only got a glimpse of him—but I'm almost certain it's——
Agnes Who? Who is it?
Maggie (*to Chris*) It's Gerry Evans, Chrissie.
Chris Christ Almighty.
Maggie He's at the bend in the lane.
Chris Oh, Jesus Christ Almighty.

*The news throws the sisters into chaos. Only Chris stands absolutely still, too
shocked to move. Agnes picks up her knitting and works with excessive
concentration. Rose and Maggie change their footwear. Everybody dashes*

about in confusion—peering into the tiny mirror, bumping into one another,
peeping out the window, combing hair. During all this hectic activity they talk
over each other and weave around the immobile Chris. The lines overlap

Kate How dare Mr Evans show his face here.
Maggie He wants to see his son, doesn't he?
Kate There's no welcome for that creature here.
Rose Who hid my Sunday shoes?
Maggie We'll have to give him his tea.
Kate I don't see why we should.
Maggie And there's nothing in the house.
Kate No business at all coming here and upsetting everybody.
Rose You're right, Kate. I hate him!
Maggie Has anybody got spare shoelaces?
Kate Look at the state of that floor.
Maggie Maybe he just wants to meet Father Jack.
Kate Father Jack may have something to say to Mr Evans. (*Of the ironing*)
    Agnes, put those clothes away.

Agnes does not hear her, so apparently engrossed is she in her knitting

Maggie My Woodbine! Where's my Woodbine?
Rose He won't stay the night, Kate, will he?
Kate He most certainly won't stay the night in this house!
Maggie Have you a piece of cord, Aggie? Anybody got a bit of twine?
Kate Behave quite normally. Be very calm and very dignified. Stop peeping
    out, Rose!
Rose (*at the window*) There's nobody coming at all.

Silence. Then Agnes puts down her knitting, rushes to the window, pushes Rose
aside and looks out

Agnes Let me see.
Rose You imagined it, Maggie.
Chris Oh God.
Rose He's not there at all.
Agnes (*softly*) Yes, he is. Maggie's right. There he is.
Rose Show me.
Kate Has he a walking stick?
Rose Yes.
Kate And a straw hat?
Rose Yes.
Kate It's Mr Evans all right.
Agnes Yes. There he is.
Chris Oh sweet God—look at the state of me—what'll I say to him—how
    close is he?
Rose I couldn't look that man in the face. I just hate him—hate him!
Kate That's a very unchristian thing to say, Rose.

Rose rushes off

There's no luck in talk like that!

Chris Look at my hands, Kate—I'm shaking.

Kate catches her shoulders

Kate You are not shaking. You are perfectly calm and you are looking beautiful and what you are going to do is this. You'll meet him outside. You'll tell him his son is healthy and happy. And then you'll send him packing—yourself and Michael are managing quite well without him—as you always have.

Chris does not move. She is about to cry. Kate now takes her in her arms

Of course ask him in. And give the creature his tea. And stay the night if he wants to. (*Firm again*) But in the outside loft. And alone. Now. I brought a newspaper home with me. Did anybody see where I left it?

Chris now rushes to the mirror and adroitly adjusts her hair and her clothes

Agnes Where is he, Maggie?

Maggie In the garden.

Kate Agnes, did you see where I left the paper?

Maggie It's on the turf box, Kate.

Kate reads the paper—or pretends to. Agnes sits beside the radio and knits with total concentration. Maggie stands at the side of the garden window

Gerry Evans enters L, *his step jaunty, swinging his cane, his straw hat well back on his head. He knows he is being watched. Although he is very ill at ease the smile never leaves his face*

Chris goes out to the garden where they meet. Gerry has an English accent

Gerry How are you, Chrissie? Great to see you.

Chris Hello, Gerry.

Gerry And how have you been for the past six months?

Chris Thirteen months.

Gerry Thirteen? Never!

Chris July last year; July the seventh.

Gerry Wow-wow-wow-wow. Where does the time go? Thirteen months? Phew! A dozen times—two dozen times I planned a visit and then something turned up and I couldn't get away.

Chris Well, you're here now.

Gerry Certainly am. And that was a bit of good fortune. Last night in a bar in Sligo. Bump into this chappie with a brand new Morris Cowley who lets slip that he's heading for Ballybeg in the morning. Ballybeg? Something familiar about that name! So. Here I am. In the flesh. As a matter of interest. Bit of good luck that, wasn't it?

Chris Yes.

Gerry He just let it slip. And here I am. Oh, yes, wonderful luck.

Chris Yes.

Pause

Maggie Looks terrified, the poor fella.

Kate Terrified, my foot.
Maggie Come here till you see him, Aggie.
Agnes Not just now.
Maggie I'm sure he could do with a good meal.
Kate I'll give him three minutes. Then if she doesn't hunt him, I will.
Gerry You're looking wonderful, Chrissie. Really great. Terrific.
Chris My hair's like a whin-bush.
Gerry Looks lovely to me.
Chris Maggie's going to wash it tonight.
Gerry And how's Maggie?
Chris Fine.
Gerry And Rose and Kate?
Chris Grand.
Gerry And Agnes?
Chris Everybody's well, thanks.
Gerry Tell her I was asking for her—Agnes.
Chris I would ask you in but the place is——
Gerry No, no, some other time; thanks all the same. The old schedule's a bit tight today. And the chappie who gave me the lift tells me Father Jack's home.
Chris Just a few weeks ago.
Gerry All the way from Africa.
Chris Yes.
Gerry Safe and sound.
Chris Yes.
Gerry Terrific.
Chris Yes.
Gerry Lucky man.
Chris Yes.

Gerry uses the cane as a golf club and swings

Gerry Must take up some exercise. Putting on too much weight.
Kate He's not still there, is he?
Maggie Yes.
Kate Doing what, in God's name?
Maggie Talking.
Kate Would someone please tell me what they have to say to each other?
Maggie He's Michael's father, Kate.
Kate That's a responsibility never burdened Mr Evans.
Chris A commercial traveller called into Kate's school last Easter. He had met you somewhere in Dublin. He had some stupid story about you giving dancing lessons up there.
Gerry He was right.
Chris He was not, Gerry!
Gerry Cross the old ticker.
Chris Real lessons?
Gerry All last winter.
Chris What sort of dancing?
Gerry Strictly ballroom. You're the one should have been giving them—

you were always far better than me. Don't you remember? (*He does a quick step and a pirouette*) Oh, that was fun while it lasted. I enjoyed that.
Chris And people came to you to be taught?
Gerry Don't look so surprised! Everybody wants to dance. I had thousands of pupils—millions!
Chris Gerry——
Gerry Fifty-three. I'm a liar. Fifty-one. And when the good weather came, they all drifted away. Shame, really. Yes, I enjoyed that. But I've just started a completely new career, as a matter of interest. Never been busier. Gramophone salesman. Agent for the whole country, if you don't mind. "Minerva Gramophones—The Wise Buy".
Chris Sounds good, Gerry.
Gerry Fabulous. All I have to do is get the orders and pass them on to Dublin. A big enterprise, Chrissie; oh, one very big enterprise.
Chris And it's going all right for you?
Gerry Unbelievable. The wholesaler can't keep up with me. Do you see this country? This country is gramophone crazy. Give you an example. Day before yesterday; just west of Oughterard; spots this small house up on the side of a hill. Something seemed just right about it—you know? Off the bike; up the lane; knocks. Out comes this enormous chappie with red hair—what are you laughing at?
Chris Gerry——
Gerry I promise you. I show him the brochures; we talk about them for ten minutes; and just like that he takes four—one for himself and three for the married daughters.
Chris He took four gramophones?
Gerry Four brochures!

They both laugh

But he'll buy. I promise you he'll buy. Tell you this, Chrissie: people thought gramophones would be a thing of the past when radios came in. But they were wrong. In my experience . . . Don't turn round; but he's watching us from behind that bush.
Chris Michael?
Gerry Pretend you don't notice. Just carry on. This all his stuff?
Chris He's making kites if you don't mind.
Gerry Unbelievable. Got a glimpse of him down at the foot of the lane. He is just enormous.
Chris He's at school, you know.
Gerry Never! Wow-wow-wow-wow. Since when?
Chris Since Christmas. Kate got him in early.
Gerry Fabulous. And he likes it?
Chris He doesn't say much.
Gerry He loves it. He adores it. They all love school nowadays. And he'll be brilliant at school. Actually I intended bringing him something small——
Chris No, no; his aunts have him——
Gerry Just a token, really. As a matter of interest I was looking at a bicycle in Kilkenny last Monday. But they only had it in blue and I thought black

might be more—you know—manly. They took my name and all. Call
next time I'm down there. Are you busy yourself?
Chris Oh, the usual—housework—looking after his lordship.
Gerry Wonderful.
Chris Give Agnes and Rose a hand at their knitting. The odd bit of sewing.
Pity you don't sell sewing-machines.
Gerry That's an idea! Do the two jobs together! Make an absolute fortune.
You have the most unbelievable business head, Chrissie. Never met
anything like it.

She laughs

What are you laughing at?
Maggie You should see the way she's looking at him—you'd think he was
the biggest toff in the world.
Kate Tinker, more likely! Loafer! Wastrel!
Maggie She knows all that, too.
Kate Too? That's all there is.
Maggie Come over till you see them, Agnes.
Agnes Not just now.
Gerry You'd never guess what I met on the road out from the town. Talk
about good luck! A cow with a single horn coming straight out of the
middle of its forehead.
Chris You never did!
Gerry As God is my judge. Walking along by itself. Nobody near it.
Chris Gerry——
Gerry And just as I was passing it, it stopped and looked me straight in the
eye.
Chris That was no cow you met—that was a unicorn.
Gerry Go ahead and mock. A unicorn has the body of a horse. This was a
cow—a perfectly ordinary brown cow except that it had a single horn just
here. Would I tell you a lie?

Chris laughs

Go ahead. Laugh. But that's what I saw. Wasn't that a spot of good luck?
Chris Was it?
Gerry A cow with a single horn? Oh, yes, that must be a good omen. How
many cows like that have you ever met?
Chris Thousands. Millions.
Gerry Stop that! I'm sure it's the only one in Ireland; maybe the only one in
the world. And I met it on the road to Ballybeg. And it winked at me.
Chris You never mentioned that.
Gerry What?
Chris That it winked at you.
Gerry Unbelievable. That's what made it all so mysterious. Oh, yes, that
must be a fabulous omen. Maybe this week I'm going to sell a gramo-
phone or two after all.
Chris But I thought you——?
Gerry Look! A single magpie! That's definitely a bad omen—one for

sorrow. (*His stick as a gun*) Bang! Missed. (*Mock serious*) Where's my
lucky cow? Come back, brown cow, come back!

They both laugh

Kate They're not *still* talking, are they?
Maggie Laughing. She laughs all the time with him. D'you hear them,
Aggie?
Agnes Yes.
Kate Laughing? Absolutely beyond my comprehension.
Agnes Like so many things, Kate.
Kate Two more minutes and Mr Evans is going to talk to me. Laughing?
Hah!
Gerry Thinking of going away for a while, Chrissie.
Chris Where to?
Gerry But I'll come back to say goodbye first.
Chris Are you going home to Wales?
Gerry Wales isn't my home any more. My home is here—well, Ireland. To
Spain—as a matter of interest. Just for a short while.
Chris To sell gramophones?
Gerry Good God, no! (*He laughs*) You'll never believe this—to do a spot of
fighting. With the International Brigade. A company leaves in a few
weeks. Bit ridiculous, isn't it? But you know old Gerry when the blood's
up—bang-bang-bang!—missing everybody.
Chris Are you serious?
Gerry Bit surprised myself—as a matter of interest.
Chris What do you know about Spain?
Gerry Not a lot. A little. Enough, maybe. Yes, I know enough. And I
thought I should try my hand at something worthy for a change. Give
Evans a Big Cause and he won't let you down. It's only everyday stuff he's
not so successful at. Anyhow I've still to enlist . . . He's still watching us.
He thinks we don't see him. I wouldn't mind talking to him.
Chris He's a bit shy.
Gerry Naturally. And I'm a stranger to him practically . . . does he know
my name?
Chris Of course he knows your name.
Gerry Good. Thanks. Well, maybe not so good. He's a very handsome
child. With your eyes. Lucky boy.

An appropriate song of the period plays softly from the radio

Maggie Good for you, Aggie. What did you do to it?
Agnes I didn't touch it.
Kate Turn that thing off, Aggie, would you?

Agnes does not

Gerry You have a gramophone! I could have got it for you wholesale.
Chris It's a wireless set.
Gerry Oh, very posh.
Chris It doesn't go half the time. Aggie says it's a heap of junk.

Gerry I know nothing about radios but I'll take a look at it if you——
Chris Some other time. When you come back.

Pause

Gerry And Agnes is well?
Chris Fine—fine.
Gerry Of all your sisters Agnes was the one who seemed to object least to
me. Tell her I was asking for her.
Chris I'll tell her.

They listen to the music

Gerry Good tune.

Suddenly he takes her in his arms and dances

Chris Gerry——
Gerry Don't talk.
Chris What are you at?
Gerry Not a word.
Chris Oh God, Gerry——
Gerry Shhh.
Chris They're watching us.
Gerry Who is?
Chris Maggie and Aggie. From the kitchen window.
Gerry Hope so. And Kate.
Chris And Father Jack.
Gerry Better still! Terrific!

*He suddenly swings her round and round and dances her lightly, elegantly
across the garden. As he does so he sings the song to her*

Maggie (*quietly*) They're dancing.
Kate What!
Maggie They're dancing together.
Kate God forgive you!
Maggie He has her in his arms.
Kate He has not! The animal! (*She flings the paper aside and joins Maggie at
the window*)
Maggie They're dancing round the garden, Aggie.
Kate Oh God, what sort of fool is she?
Maggie He's a beautiful dancer, isn't he?
Kate He's leading her astray again, Maggie.
Maggie Look at her face—she's easy led. Come here till you see, Aggie.
Agnes I'm busy! For God's sake can't you see I'm busy!

Maggie turns and looks at her in amazement

Kate That's the only thing that Evans creature could ever do well—was
dance. (*Pause*) And look at her, the fool. For God's sake, would you look
at that fool of a woman? (*Pause*) Her whole face alters when she's happy,

doesn't it? (*Pause*) They dance so well together. They're such a beautiful couple. (*Pause*) She's as beautiful as Bernie O'Donnell any day, isn't she?

Maggie moves slowly away from the window and sits motionless

Gerry Do you know the words?

Chris I never know any words.

Gerry Neither do I. Doesn't matter. This is more important. (*Pause*) Marry me, Chrissie. (*Pause*) Are you listening to me?

Chris I hear you.

Gerry Will you marry me when I come back in two weeks?

Chris I don't think so, Gerry.

Gerry I'm mad about you. You know I am. I've always been mad about you.

Chris When you're with me.

Gerry Leave this house and come away with——

Chris But you'd walk out on me again. You wouldn't intend to but that's what would happen because that's your nature and you can't help yourself.

Gerry Not this time, Chrissie. This time it will be——

Chris Don't talk any more; no more words. Just dance me down the lane and then you'll leave.

Gerry Believe me, Chrissie; this time the omens are terrific! The omens are unbelievable this time!

They dance off

After they have exited the music continues for a few seconds and then stops suddenly in mid-phrase. Maggie goes to the set, slaps it, turns it off. Kate moves away from the window

Kate They're away. Dancing.

Maggie Whatever's wrong with it, that's all it seems to last—a few minutes at a time. Something to do with the way it heats up.

Kate We probably won't see Mr Evans for another year—until the humour suddenly takes him again.

Agnes He has a Christian name.

Kate And in the meantime it's Christina's heart that gets crushed again. That's what I mind. But what really infuriates me is that the creature has no sense of ordinary duty. Does he ever wonder how she clothes and feeds Michael? Does he ask her? Does he care?

Agnes rises and goes to the back door

Agnes Going out to get my head cleared. Bit of a headache all day.

Kate Seems to me the beasts of the field have more concern for their young than that creature has.

Agnes Do you ever listen to yourself, Kate? You are such a damned righteous bitch! And his name is Gerry!—Gerry!—Gerry!

Now on the point of tears, Agnes runs off

Kate And what was that all about?

Maggie Who's to say?
Kate Don't I know his name is Gerry? What am I calling him?—St Patrick?
Maggie She's worried about Chris, too.
Kate You see, that's what a creature like Mr Evans does: appears out of
nowhere and suddenly poisons the atmosphere in the whole house—God
forgive him, the bastard! There! That's what I mean! God forgive me!

*Maggie begins putting on her long-laced boots again. As she does she sings
listlessly, almost inaudibly*

Maggie   " 'Twas on the Isle of Capri that he found her
                 Beneath the shade of an old walnut tree.
                 Oh, I can still see the flowers blooming round her,
                 Where they met on the Isle of Capri."
Kate If you knew your prayers as well as you know the words of those aul
pagan songs! . . . She's right: I am a righteous bitch, amn't I?
Maggie   "She was as sweet as a rose at the dawning
                 But somehow fate hadn't meant it to be,
                 And though he sailed with the tide in the morning,
                 Still his heart's in the Isle of Capri."
(She now stands up and looks at her feet) Now. Who's for a fox-trot?
Kate You work hard at your job. You try to keep the home together. You
perform your duties as best you can—because you believe in responsibilities and obligations and good order. And then suddenly, suddenly you
realize that hair cracks are appearing everywhere; that control is slipping
away; that the whole thing is so fragile it can't be held together much
longer. It's all about to collapse, Maggie.
Maggie *(wearily)* Nothing's about to collapse, Kate.
Kate That young Sweeney boy from the back hills—the boy who was
anointed   his trousers didn't catch fire, as Rose said. They were doing
some devilish thing with a goat—some sort of sacrifice for the Lughnasa
Festival; and Sweeney was so drunk he toppled over into the middle of the
bonfire. Don't know why that came into my head . . .
Maggie Kate . . . *(She goes to her and sits beside her)*
Kate And Mr Evans is off again for another twelve months and next week
or the week after Christina'll collapse into one of her depressions.
Remember last winter?—all that sobbing and lamenting in the middle of
the night. I don't think I could go through that again. And the doctor says
he doesn't think Father Jack's mind is confused but that his superiors
probably had no choice but send him home. Whatever he means by that,
Maggie. And the parish priest did talk to me today. He said the numbers
in the school are falling and that there may not be a job for me after the
summer. But the numbers aren't falling, Maggie. Why is he telling me lies?
Why does he want rid of me? And why has he never come out to visit
Father Jack? *(She tries to laugh)* If he gives me the push, all five of us will
be at home together all day long—we can spend the day dancing to
Marconi.

Now she cries. Maggie puts her arms around her

Michael enters L

But what worries me most of all is Rose. If I died—if I lost my job—if this
house were broken up—what would become of our Rosie?
Maggie Shhh.
Kate I must put my trust in God, Maggie, mustn't I? He'll look after her,
won't he? You believe that, Maggie, don't you?
Maggie Kate ... Kate ... Kate, love ...
Kate I believe that, too ... I believe that ... I do believe that ...

Maggie holds her and rocks her

*Chris enters quickly L, hugging herself. She sees the boy at his kites, goes to
him and gets down beside him. She speaks eagerly, excitedly, confidentially*

Chris Well. Now you've had a good look at him. What do you think of
him? Do you remember him?
Boy (*bored*) I never saw him before.
Chris Shhh. Yes, you did; five or six times. You've forgotten. And he saw
you at the foot of the lane. He thinks you've got very big. And he thinks
you're handsome!
Boy Aunt Kate got me a spinning-top that won't spin.
Chris He's handsome. Isn't he handsome?
Boy Give up.
Chris I'll tell you a secret. The others aren't to know. He has got a great new
job! And he's wonderful at it!
Boy What does he do?
Chris Shhh. And he has bought a bicycle for you—a black bike—a man's
bike and he's going to bring it with him the next time he comes. (*She
suddenly embraces him and hugs him*)
Boy Is he coming back soon?
Chris (*eyes closed*) Maybe—maybe. Yes! Yes, he is!
Boy How soon?
Chris Next week—the week after—soon—soon—soon! Oh, yes, you have a
handsome father. You are a lucky boy and I am a very, very lucky
woman. (*She gets to her feet, then bends down again and kisses him lightly*)
And another bit of good news for you, lucky boy: you have your mother's
eyes! (*She laughs, pirouettes flirtatiously before him and dances into the
kitchen*) And what's the good news here?
Maggie The good news here is ... that's the most exciting turf we've ever
burned!
Kate Gerry's not gone, is he?
Chris Just this minute.

Agnes enters through the back door. She is carrying some roses

He says to thank you very much for the offer of the bed.
Kate Next time he's back.
Chris That'll be in a week or two—depending on his commitments.
Kate Well, if the outside loft happens to be empty.
Chris And he sends his love to you all. His special love to you, Aggie; and a
big kiss.
Agnes For me?

Chris Yes! For you!

Maggie (*quickly*) Those are beautiful, Aggie. Would Jack like some in his room? Put them on his windowsill with a wee card—"ROSES"—so that the poor man's head won't be demented looking for the word. And now, girls, the daily dilemma: what's for tea?

Chris Let me make the tea, Maggie.

Maggie We'll both make the tea. Perhaps something thrilling with tomatoes? We've got two, I think. Or if you're prepared to wait, I'll get that soda-bread made.

Agnes I'm making the tea, Maggie.

Chris Let me, please. Just today.

Agnes (*almost aggressively*) I make the tea every evening, don't I? Why shouldn't I make it this evening as usual?

Maggie No reason at all. Aggie's the chef. (*She sings raucously*)
"Everybody's doing it, doing it, doing it.
Picking their noses and chewing it, chewing it, chewing it . . ."

Kate Maggie, please!

Maggie If she knew her prayers half as well as she knows the words of those aul pagan songs . . . (*Now at the radio*) Marconi, my friend, you're not still asleep, are you?

Father Jack enters. He shuffles quickly across the kitchen floor, hands behind his back, eyes on the ground, as if he were intent on some engagement elsewhere. Now he becomes aware of the others

Jack If anybody is looking for me, I'll be down at the bank of the river for the rest of the . . . (*He tails off and looks around. Now he knows where he is. He smiles*) I beg your pardon. My mind was . . . It's Kate.

Kate It's Kate.

Jack And Agnes. And Margaret.

Maggie How are you, Jack?

Jack And this is —?

Chris Chris—Christina.

Jack Forgive me, Chris. You were only a baby when I went away. I remember Mother lifting you up as the train was pulling out of the station and catching your hand and waving it at me. You were so young you had scarcely any hair but she had managed to attach a tiny pink—a tiny pink—what's the word—a bowl—a bowl—just about here; and as she waved her hand, the bow fell off. It's like a—a picture?—a camera-picture?—a photograph!—it's like a photograph in my mind.

Chris The hair isn't much better even now, Jack.

Jack And I remember you crying, Margaret.

Maggie Was I?

Jack Yes; your face was all blotchy with tears.

Maggie You may be sure—beautiful as ever.

Jack (*to Agnes*) And you and Kate were on Mother's right and Rose was between you; you each had a hand. And Mother's face, I remember, showed nothing. I often wondered about that afterwards.

Chris She knew she would never see you again in her lifetime.
Jack I know that. But in the other life. Do you think perhaps Mother didn't
believe in the ancestral spirits?
Kate Ancestral . . . ! What are you blathering about, Jack? Mother was a
saintly women who knew she was going straight to heaven. And don't you
forget to take your medicine again this evening. You're supposed to take
it three times a day.
Jack One of our priests took so much quinine that he became an addict and
almost died. A German priest; Father Sharpeggi. He was rushed to
hospital in Kampala but they could do nothing for him. So Okawa and I
brought him to our local medicine man and Karl Sharpeggi lived until he
was eighty-eight! There was a strange white bird on my windowsill when I
woke up this morning.
Agnes That's Rosie's pet rooster. Keep away from that thing.
Maggie Look what it did to my arm, Jack. One of these days I'm going to
wring its neck.
Jack That's what we do in Ryanga when we want to please the spirits—or
to appease them: we kill a rooster or a young goat. It's a very exciting
exhibition—that's not the word, is it?—demonstration?—no—show? No,
no; what's the word I'm looking for? Spectacle? That's not it. The word to
describe a sacred and mysterious . . . ? (*Slowly, deliberately*) You have a
ritual killing. You offer up sacrifice. You have dancing and incantations.
What is the name for that whole—for that—? Gone. Lost it. My
vocabulary has deserted me. Never mind. Doesn't matter . . . I think
perhaps I should put on more clothes . . .

Pause

Maggie Did you speak Swahili all the time out there, Jack?
Jack All the time. Yes. To the people. Swahili. When Europeans call, we
speak English. Or if we have a—a visitor?—a visitation!—from the
district commissioner. The present commissioner knows Swahili but
won't speak it. He's a stubborn man. He and I fight a lot but I like him.
The Irish Outcast, he calls me. He is always inviting me to spend a
weekend with him in Kampala—to keep me from "going native", as he
calls it. Perhaps when I go back. If you co-operate with the English they
give you lots of money for churches and schools and hospitals. And he
gets so angry with me because I won't take his money. Reported me to my
superiors in Head House last year; and they were very cross—oh, very
cross. But I like him. When I was saying goodbye to him—he thought this
was very funny!—he gave me a present of the last governor's ceremonial
hat to take home with—Ceremony! That's the word! How could I have
forgotten that? The offering, the ritual, the dancing—a ceremony! Such a
simple word. What was I telling you?
Agnes The district commissioner gave you this present.
Jack Yes; a wonderful triangular hat with three enormous white ostrich
plumes rising up out of the crown. I have it in one of my trunks. I'll show
it to you later. Ceremony! I'm so glad I got that. Do you know what I
found very strange? Coming back in the boat there were days when I

couldn't remember even the simplest words. Not that anybody seemed to notice. And you can always point, Margaret, can't you?

Maggie Or make signs.

Jack Or make signs.

Maggie Or dance.

Kate What you must do is read a lot—books, papers, magazines, anything. I read every night with young Michael. It's great for his vocabulary.

Jack I'm sure you're right, Kate. I'll do that. (*To Chris*) I haven't seen young Michael today, Agnes.

Kate Christina, Jack.

Jack Sorry, I——

Chris He's around there somewhere. Making kites, if you don't mind.

Jack And I have still to meet your husband.

Chris I'm not married.

Jack Ah.

Kate Michael's father was here a while ago . . . Gerry Evans . . . Mr Evans is a Welshman . . . not that that's relevant to . . .

Jack You were never married?

Chris Never.

Maggie We're all in the same boat, Jack. We're hoping that you'll hunt about and get men for all of us.

Jack (*to Chris*) So Michael is a love-child?

Chris I—yes—I suppose so . . .

Jack He's a fine boy.

Chris He's not a bad boy

Jack You're lucky to have him.

Agnes We're all lucky to have him.

Jack In Ryanga women are eager to have love-children. The more love-children you have, the more fortunate your household is thought to be. Have you other love-children?

Kate She certainly has not, Jack; and strange as it may seem to you, neither has Agnes nor Rose nor Maggie nor myself. No harm to Ryanga but you're home in Donegal now and much as we cherish love-children here they are not exactly the norm. And the doctors says if you don't take exercise your legs will seize up on you; so I'm going to walk you down to the main road and up again three times and then you'll get your tea and then you'll read the paper from front to back and then you'll take your medicine and then you'll go to bed. And we'll do the same thing tomorrow and the day after and the day after that until we have you back to what you were. You start off and I'll be with you in a second. Where's my cardigan?

Jack goes out to the garden. Kate gets her cardigan

Michael Some of Aunt Kate's forebodings weren't all that inaccurate. Indeed some of them were fulfilled before the Festival of Lughnasa was over.

   She was right about Uncle Jack. He had been sent home by his superiors, not because his mind was confused, but for reasons that became clearer as the summer drew to a close. And she was right about losing her job in the local school. The parish priest didn't take her back when the new term began; although that had more to do with Father Jack than with falling numbers.

And she had good reason for being uneasy about Rose—and, had she known, about Agnes, too. But what she couldn't have foreseen was that the home would break up quite so quickly and that when she would wake up one morning in early September both Rose and Agnes would have left for ever.

At this point in Michael's speech Jack picks up two pieces of wood, portions of the kites, and strikes them together. The sound they make pleases him. He does it again—and again—and again. Now he begins to beat out a structured beat whose rhythm gives him pleasure. And as Michael continues his speech, Jack begins to shuffle-dance in time to his tattoo—his body slightly bent over, his eyes on the ground, his feet moving rhythmically. And as he dances—shuffles, he mutters—sings—makes occasional sounds that are incomprehensible and almost inaudible. Kate comes out to the garden and stands still, watching him

Rose enters

Now Rose and Maggie and Agnes are all watching him—some at the front door, some through the window. Only Chris has her eyes closed, her face raised, her mouth slightly open; remembering. Michael continues without stopping

But she was wrong about my father. I suppose their natures were so out of tune that she would always be wrong about my father. Because he did come back in a couple of weeks as he said he would. And although my mother and he didn't go through a conventional form of marriage, once more they danced together, witnessed by the unseen sisters. And this time it was a dance without music; just there, in ritual circles round and round that square and then down the lane and back up again; slowly, formally, with easy deliberation. My mother with her head thrown back, her eyes closed, her mouth slightly open. My father holding her just that little distance away from him so that he could regard her upturned face. No singing, no melody, no words. Only the swish and whisper of their feet across the grass.

I watched the ceremony from behind that bush. But this time they were conscious only of themselves and of their dancing. And when he went off to fight with the International Brigade, my mother grieved as any bride would grieve. But this time there was no sobbing, no lamenting, no collapse into a depression.

Kate now goes to Jack and gently takes the sticks from him. She places them on the ground

Kate We'll leave these back where we found them, Jack. They aren't ours. They belong to the child.

She takes his arm and leads him off

Now we'll go for our walk.

The others watch with expressionless faces

CURTAIN

ACT II

The same. Early September; three weeks later

There is an ink bottle and some paper on the kitchen table. Two finished kites—their artwork still unseen—lean against the garden seat

Michael stands DL, listening to Maggie as she approaches, singing. Now she enters L carrying two zinc buckets of water. She is dressed as she was in Act I. She sings in her usual parodic style

Maggie   "Oh play to me, Gypsy;
The moon's high above.
Oh, play me your serenade,
The song I love . . ."
(*She goes into the kitchen and from her zinc buckets she fills the kettle and the saucepan on the range. She looks over at the writing materials*) Are you getting your books ready for school again?

Boy School doesn't start for another ten days.

Maggie God, I always hated school. (*She hums the next line of the song. Then she remembers*) You and I have a little financial matter to discuss. (*Pause*) D'you hear me, cub?

Boy I'm not listening.

Maggie You owe me money.

Boy I do not.

Maggie Oh, yes, you do. Three weeks ago I bet you a penny those aul kites would never get off the ground. And they never did.

Boy Because there was never enough wind; that's why.

Maggie Enough wind! Would you listen to him. A hurricane wouldn't shift those things. Anyway a debt is a debt. One penny please at your convenience. Or the equivalent in kind: one Wild Woodbine.
(*Singing*)   "Beside your caravan
The campfire's bright . . ."
(*She dances her exaggerated dance across to the table and tousles the Boy's hair*)

Boy Leave me alone, Aunt Maggie.

Maggie   "I'll be your vagabond
Just for tonight . . ."

Boy Now look at what you made me do! The page is all blotted!

Maggie Your frank opinion, cub: am I vagabond material?

Boy Get out of my road, will you? I'm trying to write a letter.

Maggie Who to? That's for me to know and you to find out. Whoever it is, he'd need to be smart to read that scrawl. (*She returns to her buckets*)

Boy It's to Santa Claus.

Maggie In September? Nothing like getting in before the rush. What are you asking for?
Boy A bell.
Maggie A bell.
Boy For my bicycle.
Maggie For your bicycle.
Boy The bike my daddy has bought me—stupid!
Maggie Your daddy has bought you a bicycle?
Boy He told me today. He bought it in Kilkenny. So there!

Her manner changes. She returns to the table

Maggie (*softly*) Your daddy told you that?
Boy Ask him yourself. It's coming next week. It's a black bike—a man's bike.
Maggie Aren't you the lucky boy?
Boy It's going to be delivered here to the house. He promised me.
Maggie Well, if he promised you . . . (*Very brisk*) Now! Who can we get to teach you to ride?
Boy I know how to ride!
Maggie You don't.
Boy I learned at school last Easter. So there! But you can't ride.
Maggie I can so.
Boy I know you can't.
Maggie Maybe not by myself. But put me on the bar, cub—magnificent!
Boy You never sat on the bar of a bike in your life, Aunt Maggie!
Maggie Oh yes, I did, Michael. Oh yes, indeed I did. (*She gathers up the papers*) Now away and write to Santa some other time. On a day like this you should be out running about the fields like a young calf. Hold on a new riddle for you.
Boy Give up.
Maggie A man goes to an apple tree with two apples on it. He doesn't take apples off it. He doesn't leave apples on it. How does he do that?
Boy Give up.
Maggie Think, will you!
Boy Give up.
Maggie Well, since you don't know, I will tell you. He takes *one* apple off! Get it? He doesn't take *apples* off! He doesn't leave *apples* on!
Boy God!
Maggie You might as well be talking to a turf stack.

Jack enters. He looks much stronger and is very sprightly and alert. He is not wearing the top coat or the hat but instead a garish-coloured—probably a sister's—sweater. His dress looks now even more bizarre

Jack Did I hear the church bell ringing?
Maggie A big posh wedding today.
Jack Not one of my sisters?
Maggie No such luck. A man called Austin Morgan and a girl from Carrickfad.
Jack Austin Morgan—should I know that name?

Maggie I don't think so. They own the Arcade in the town. And how are you today?

Jack Cold as usual, Maggie. And complaining about it as usual.

Michael exits

Maggie Complain away—why wouldn't you? And it is getting colder. But you're looking stronger every day, Jack.

Jack I feel stronger, too. Now! Off for my last walk of the day.

Maggie Number three?

Jack Number four! Down past the clothes line; across the stream; round the old well; and up through the meadow. And when that's done Kate won't have to nag at me—nag?—nag?—sounds funny—something wrong with that—nag?—that's not a word, is it?

Maggie Nag—yes; to keep on at somebody.

Jack Yes? Nag. Good. So my English vocabulary is coming back, too. Great. Nag. Still sounds a bit strange.

Kate enters with an armful of clothes from the clothes line

Kate Time for another walk, Jack.

Jack Just about to set out on number four, Kate. And thank you for keeping at me.

Kate No sign of Rose and Agnes yet?

Maggie They said they'd be back for tea. (*To Jack*) They're away picking bilberries.

Kate (*to Jack*) You used to pick bilberries. Do you remember?

Jack Down beside the old quarry?

Maggie The very place.

Jack Mother and myself; every Lughnasa; the annual ritual. Of course I remember. And then she'd make the most wonderful jam. And that's what you took to school with you every day all through the winter: a piece of soda bread and bilberry jam.

Maggie But no butter.

Jack Except on special occasions when you got scones and for some reason they were always buttered. I must walk down to that old quarry one of these days.
"O ruddier than the cherry,
O sweeter than the berry,
O nymph more bright,
Than moonshine night,
Like kidlings blithe and merry."
(*He laughs*) Where on earth did that come from? You see, Kate, it's all coming back to me.

Kate So you'll soon begin saying Mass again?

Jack Yes, indeed.

Maggie Here in the house?

Jack Why not? Perhaps I'll start next Monday. The neighbours would join us, wouldn't they?

Kate They surely would. A lot of them have been asking me already.

Jack How will we let them know?
Maggie I wouldn't worry about that. Word gets about very quickly.
Jack What Okawa does—you know Okawa, don't you?
Maggie Your house boy?
Jack My friend—my mentor—my counsellor—and yes, my house boy as well; anyhow Okawa summons our people by striking a huge iron gong. Did you hear that wedding bell this morning, Kate?
Kate Yes.
Jack Well, Okawa's gong would carry four times as far as that. But if it's one of the bigger ceremonies, he'll spend a whole day going round all the neighbouring villages, blowing on this enormous flute he made himself.
Maggie And they all meet in your church?
Jack When I had a church. Now we gather in the common in the middle of the village. If it's an important ceremony, you would have up to three or four hundred people.
Kate All gathered together for Mass?
Jack Maybe. Or maybe to offer sacrifice to Obi, our Great Goddess of the Earth, so that the crops will flourish. Or maybe to get in touch with our departed fathers for their advice and wisdom. Or maybe to thank the spirits of our tribe if they have been good to us; or to appease them if they're angry. I complain to Okawa that our calendar of ceremonies gets fuller every year. Now at this time of year over there—at the Ugandan harvest time—we have two very wonderful ceremonies: the Festival of the New Yam and the Festival of the Sweet Cassava; and they're both dedicated to our Great Goddess, Obi——
Kate But these aren't Christian ceremonies, Jack, are they?
Jack Oh, no. The Ryangans have always been faithful to their own beliefs—like these two Festivals I'm telling you about; and they are very special, really magnificent ceremonies. I haven't described those two Festivals to you before, have I?
Kate Not to me.
Jack Well, they begin very formally, very solemnly with the ritual sacrifice of a fowl or a goat or a calf down at the bank of the river. Then the ceremonial cutting and anointing of the first yams and the first cassava; and we pass these round in huge wooden bowls. Then the incantation—a chant, really—that expresses our gratitude and that also acts as a rhythm or percussion for the ritual dance. And then, when the thanksgiving is over, the dance continues. And the interesting thing is that it grows naturally into a secular celebration; so that almost imperceptibly the religious ceremony ends and the community celebration takes over. And that part of the ceremony is a real spectacle. We light fires round the periphery of the circle; and we paint our faces with coloured powders; and we sing local songs; and we drink palm wine. And then we dance—and dance—and dance—children, men, women, most of them lepers, many of them with misshapen limbs, with missing limbs—dancing, believe it or not, for days on end! It is the most wonderful sight you have ever seen! (*He laughs*) That palm wine! They dole it out in horns! You lose all sense of time . . . !

Oh, yes, the Ryangans are a remarkable people: there is no distinction between the religious and the secular in their culture. And of course their capacity for fun, for laughing, for practical jokes—they've such open hearts! In some respects they're not unlike us. You'd love them, Maggie. You should come back with me!

How did I get into all that? You must stop me telling these long stories. Exercise time! I'll be back in ten minutes; and only last week it took me half an hour to do number four. You've done a great job with me, Kate. So please do keep nagging at me. (*He moves off—then stops*) It's not Gilbert and Sullivan, is it?

Kate Sorry?

Jack That quotation.

Kate What's that, Jack?

Jack "O ruddier than the cherry/O sweeter than the berry"—no, it's not Gilbert and Sullivan. But it'll come back to me, I promise you. It's all coming back. (*Again he moves off*)

Kate Jack.

Jack Yes?

Kate You are going to start saying Mass again?

Jack We've agreed on next Monday, haven't we? Haven't we, Maggie?

Maggie Yes.

Jack At first light. The moment Rose's white cock crows. A harvest ceremony. You'll have to find a big gong somewhere, Kate.

He leaves

Pause. Kate and Maggie stare at each other in concern, in alarm. They speak in hushed voices

Kate I told you—you wouldn't believe me—I told you.

Maggie Shhh.

Kate What do you think?

Maggie He's not back a month yet.

Kate Yesterday I heard about their medicine man who brought a woman back from death——

Maggie He needs more time.

Kate And this morning it was "the spirits of the tribe"! And when I mentioned Mass to him you saw how he dodged about.

Maggie He said he'd say Mass next Monday, Kate.

Kate No, he won't. You know he won't. He's changed, Maggie.

Maggie In another month, he'll be——

Kate Completely changed. He's not our Jack at all. And it's what he's changed into that frightens me.

Maggie Doesn't frighten me.

Kate If you saw your face ... of course it does ... Oh, dear God ...

Maggie now drifts back to the range. Kate goes to the table and with excessive vigour wipes it with a damp cloth. Then she stops suddenly, slumps into a seat and covers her face with her hands. Maggie watches her, then goes to her. She stands behind her and holds her shoulders with her hands. Kate grasps Maggie's hands in hers

Maggie All the same, Kitty, I don't think it's a sight I'd like to see.
Kate What sight?
Maggie A clatter of lepers trying to do the Military Two-step.
Kate God forgive you, Maggie Mundy! The poor creatures are as entitled to——

She breaks off because Chris's laughter is heard off. Kate jumps to her feet

This must be kept in the family, Maggie! Not a word of this must go outside these walls—d'you hear?—not a syllable!

Chris and Gerry enter L. *He enters backways pulling Chris who holds the end of his walking stick. Throughout the scene he keeps trying to embrace her. She keeps avoiding him*

Gerry No false modesty. You know you're a great dancer, Chrissie.
Chris No, I'm not.
Gerry You should be a professional dancer.
Chris You're talking rubbish.
Gerry Let's dance round the garden again.
Chris We've done that; and down the lane and up again—without music. And that's enough for one day. Tell me about signing up. Was it really in a church?
Gerry I'm telling you—it was unbelievable.
Chris It was a real church?
Gerry A Catholic church as a matter of interest.
Chris I don't believe a word of it.
Gerry Would I tell you a lie? And up at the end—in the sanctuary?—there were three men, two of them with trenchcoats; and between them, behind this lectern and wearing a sort of military cap, this little chappie who spoke in an accent I could hardly understand. Naturally I thought he was Spanish. From Armagh, as it turned out.
Chris I'm sure he couldn't understand you either.
Gerry He described himself as the recruiting officer. "Take it from me, comrade, nobody joins the Brigade without my unanimity."

She laughs—and avoids his embrace

Chris It's a wonder he accepted you.
Gerry "Do you offer your allegiance and your loyalty and your full endeavours to the Popular Front?"
Chris What's the Popular Front?
Gerry The Spanish government that I'm going to keep in power. "I take it you are a Syndicalist?" "No." "An Anarchist?" "No." "A Marxist?" "No." "A Republican, a Socialist, a Communist?" "No." "Do you speak Spanish?" "No." "Can you make explosives?" "No." "Can you ride a motor-bike?" "Yes." "You're in. Sign here."
Chris So you'll be a dispatch rider?

Gerry imitates riding a motor-bike

And leave on Saturday?
Gerry First tide.

Chris How long will you be away?
Gerry As long as it takes to sort the place out.
Chris Seriously, Gerry.
Gerry Maybe a couple of months. Everybody says it will be over by Christmas.
Chris They always say it will be over by Christmas. I still don't know why you're going.
Gerry Not sure I know either. Who wants salesmen that can't sell? And there's bound to be *something* right about the cause, isn't there? And it's somewhere to go—isn't it? Maybe that's the important thing for a man: a *named* destination—democracy, Ballybeg, heaven. Women's illusions aren't so easily satisfied—they make better drifters. (*He laughs*) Anyhow he held out a pen to sign on the dotted line and it was only when I was writing my name that I glanced over the lectern and saw the box.
Chris What box?
Gerry He was standing on a box. The chappie was a midget!
Chris Gerry!
Gerry No bigger than three feet.
Chris Gerry, I——
Gerry Promise you! And when we were having a drink afterwards he told me he was invaluable to the Brigade—because he was a master at disguising himself!
Chris Gerry Evans, you are——
Gerry Let's go down to the old well.
Chris We're going nowhere. Come inside and take a look at this wireless. It stops and starts whenever it feels like it.
Gerry I told you: I know nothing about radios.
Chris I've said you're a genius at them.
Gerry Chrissie, I don't even know how to——
Chris You can try, can't you? Come on. Michael misses it badly.

She runs into the kitchen. He follows

You should see Jack striding through the meadow. He looks like a new man.
Kate (*to Gerry*) Were you talking to him?
Gerry He wants to do a swap with me: I'm to give him this hat and he's to give me some sort of a three-cornered hat with feathers that the district commissioner gave him. Sounds a fair exchange.
Maggie Chrissie says you're great with radios, Gerry.
Gerry I'll take a look at it—why not?
Maggie All I can tell you is that it's not the battery. I got a new one yesterday.
Gerry Let me check the aerial first. Very often that's where the trouble lies. Then I'll have a look at the ignition and sparking plugs. Leave it to Gerry.

Gerry winks at Chris as he goes out the front door and off R

Maggie He sounds very knowledgeable.
Chris It may be something he can't fix.

Kate I know you're not responsible for Gerry's decisions, Christina. But it would be on my conscience if I didn't tell you how strongly I disapprove of this International Brigade caper. It's a sorry day for Ireland when we send young men off to Spain to fight for godless Communism.

Chris For democracy, Kate.

Kate I'm not going to argue. I just want to clear my conscience.

Chris That's the important thing, of course. And now you've cleared it.

Gerry runs on

Gerry (*calling through the window*) Turn the radio on, Chrissie, would you?

Maggie It's on.

Gerry Right.

Gerry runs off again

Chris Just as we were coming out of the town we met Vera McLaughlin, the knitting agent. (*Softly*) Agnes and Rose aren't back yet?

Maggie They'll be here soon.

Chris She says she'll call in tomorrow and tell them herself. The poor woman was very distressed.

Kate Tell them what?

Chris She's not buying any more hand-made gloves.

Maggie Why not?

Chris Too dear, she says.

Kate Too dear! She pays them a pittance!

Chris There's a new factory started up in Donegal Town. They make machine gloves more quickly there and far more cheaply. The people Vera used to supply buy their gloves direct from the factory now.

Maggie That's awful news, Chrissie.

Chris She says they're organizing buses to bring the workers to the factory and back every day. Most of the people who used to work at home have signed on. She tried to get a job there herself. They told her she was too old. She's forty-one. The poor woman could hardly speak.

Maggie Oh God . . . poor Aggie . . . poor Rose . . . what'll they do?

Agnes enters the garden

Kate (*seeing Agnes*) Shhh. They're back. Let them have their tea in peace. Tell them later.

They busy themselves with their tasks. Agnes is carrying two small pails of blackberries which she leaves outside the door of the house. Just as she is about to enter the kitchen a voice off calls her

Gerry (*off*) Who is that beautiful woman!

Agnes looks around, puzzled

Agnes Gerry?

Gerry (*off*) Up here, Aggie!

Agnes Where?

Gerry (*off*) On top of the sycamore.

Now she sees him. The audience does not see him

Agnes Mother of God!

Gerry (*off*) Come up and join me!

Agnes What are you doing up there?

Gerry (*off*) You can see into the future from here, Aggie!

Agnes The tree isn't safe, Gerry. Please come down.

Gerry (*off*) Come up and see what's going to happen to you!

Agnes That branch is dead, Gerry. I'm telling you.

The branch begins to sway

Gerry (*off*) Do you think I could get a job in a circus? Wow-wow-wow-wow!

Agnes Gerry . . .!

Gerry (*off; singing*) "He flies through the air with the greatest of ease—" Wheeeeeeeeee!

She covers her eyes in terror

Agnes Stop it, Gerry, stop it, stop it!

Gerry "That daring young man on the flying trapeze . . ."

Agnes You're going to fall! I'm not looking! I'm not watching! (*She dashes into the house*) That clown of a man is up on top of the sycamore. Go out and tell him to come down, Chrissie.

Maggie He's fixing the aerial.

Agnes He's going to break his neck—I'm telling you!

Maggie As long as he fixes the wireless first.

Kate How are the bilberries, Agnes?

Agnes Just that bit too ripe. We should have picked them a week ago.

Chris Is that a purple stain on your gansey?

Agnes I know. I'd only begun when I fell into a bush. And look at my hands—all scrabbed with briars. For all the sympathy I got from Rosie. Nearly died laughing at me. How is she now? (*Pause*) Is she still in bed?

Chris Bed?

Agnes She wasn't feeling well. She left me and went home to lie down. (*Pause*) She's here, isn't she?

Maggie rushes off to the bedroom

Kate I haven't seen her. (*To Chris*) Have you?

Chris No.

Kate When did she leave you?

Agnes Hours ago—I don't know—almost immediately after we got to the old quarry. She said she felt out of sorts.

Chris And she went off by herself?

Agnes Yes.

Kate To come home?

Agnes That's what she said.

Maggie enters

Maggie She's not in bed.

Agnes Oh God! Where could she——
Kate Start at the beginning, Agnes. What exactly happened?
Agnes Nothing "happened"—nothing at all. We left here together—when was it?—just after one o'clock——
Chris That means she's missing for over three hours.
Agnes We walked together to the quarry. She was chatting away as usual. I had my two buckets and she had——
Kate Go on—go on!
Agnes And just after we got there she said she wasn't feeling well. I told her not to bother about the bilberries—just to sit in the sun. And that's what she did.
Kate For how long?
Agnes I don't know—five—ten minutes. And then I fell into the bush. And that was when she laughed. And then she said—she said—I've forgotten what she said—something about a headache and her stomach being sick and she'd go home and sleep for a while. (*To Maggie*) You're sure she's not in her bed?

Maggie shakes her head

Kate Then what?

Agnes begins to cry

Agnes Where is she? What's happened to our Rosie?
Kate What direction did she go when she left you?
Agnes Direction?
Kate Stop snivelling, Agnes! Did she go towards home?
Agnes I think so ... yes ... I don't know ... Maggie——
Maggie She may have gone into the town.
Chris She wouldn't have gone into town in her wellingtons.
Agnes She was wearing her good shoes.
Kate Are you sure?
Agnes Yes; and her blue cardigan and her good skirt. I said to her—I said, "You're some lady to go picking bilberries with." And she just laughed and said, "I'm some toff, Aggie, amn't I some toff?"
Maggie Had she a bottle of milk with her?
Agnes I think so—yes—in one of her cans.
Maggie Had she any money with her?
Agnes She had half-a-crown. That's all she has.
Maggie (*softly*) Danny Bradley.
Kate What?—who?
Maggie Danny Bradley ... Lough Anna ... up in the back hills.
Chris Oh God, no.
Kate What?—what's this?—what about the back hills?
Chris She has some silly notion about that scamp, Bradley. She believes he's in love with her. He gave her a present last Christmas—she says.
Kate (*to Agnes*) What do you know about this Bradley business?
Agnes I know no more than Chris has——
Kate I've often seen you and Rose whispering together. What plot has been hatched between Rose and Mr Bradley?

Agnes No plot ... please, Kate——
Kate You're lying to me, Agnes! You're withholding! I want the truth!
Agnes Honest to God, all I know is what Chris has just——
Kate I want to know everything you know! Now! I want to——
Maggie That'll do, Kate! Stop that at once! (*Calmly*) She may be in the
town. She may be on her way home now. She may have taken a weak turn
on her way back from the quarry. We're going to find her. (*To Chris*) You
search the fields on the upper side of the lane. (*To Agnes*) You take the
lower side, down as far as the main road. (*To Kate*) You go to the old well
and search all around there. I'm going into the town to tell the police.
Kate You're going to no police, Maggie. If she's mixed up with that Bradley
creature, I'm not going to have it broadcast all over——
Maggie I'm going to the police and you'll do what I told you to do.
Chris (*at the window*) There she is! Look—look! There she is!

*She has seen Rose and is about to rush out to greet her. Maggie catches her
arm and restrains her*

  Rose enters

*The four sisters watch Rose as she crosses the garden—Chris and Kate from
the window, Maggie and Agnes from the door. Rose is unaware of their
anxious scrutiny. She is dressed in the "good" clothes described by Agnes and
they have changed her appearance. Indeed, had we not seen the Rose of Act I,
we might not now be immediately aware of her disability. At first look this
might be any youngish country woman, carefully dressed, not unattractive,
returning from a long walk on a summer day. She walks slowly, lethargically,
towards the house. From her right hand hangs a red poppy that she plucked
casually along the road. Her face reveals nothing—but nothing is being
deliberately concealed. She sees Agnes's cans of fruit. She stops beside them
and looks at them. Then she puts her hand into one of the cans, takes a fistful of
berries and thrusts the fistful into her mouth. Then she wipes her mouth with
her sleeve and the back of her hand. As she chews she looks at her stained
fingers. She wipes them on her skirt. All of these movements—stopping, eating,
wiping—are done not dreamily, abstractedly, but calmly, naturally. Now she
moves towards the house. As she approaches the door Agnes rushes to meet
her. Instead of hugging her, as she wants to, she catches her arm*

Agnes Rosie, love, we were beginning to get worried about you.
Rose They're nice, Aggie. They're sweet. And you got two canfuls. Good
for you.

Agnes leads her into the house

Agnes Is your stomach settled?
Rose My stomach?
Agnes You weren't feeling well—remember?—when we were at the quarry?
Rose Oh yes. Oh, I'm fine now thanks.
Agnes You left me there and you said you were coming home to lie down.
D'you remember that?
Rose Yes.

Chris But you didn't come home, Rosie.

Rose That's right.

Agnes And we were worried about you.

Rose Well . . . here I am.

Chris Were you in the town?

Agnes That's why you're all dressed up, isn't it?

Chris You went into Ballybeg, didn't you?

Pause. Rose looks from one to the other

Maggie (*briskly*) She's home safe and sound and that's all that matters.
Now I don't know about you girls but I can tell you this chicken is weak
with hunger. Let me tell you what's on the menu this evening. Our
beverage is the usual hot, sweet tea. There is a choice between caraway-
seed bread and soda bread, both fresh from the chef's oven. But now we
come to the difficulty: there's only three eggs between the seven of us—I
wish to God you'd persuade that white rooster of yours to lay eggs, Rosie.

Chris There are eight of us, Maggie.

Maggie How are there . . . ? Of course—the soldier up the sycamore! Not a
great larder but a nice challenge to someone like myself. Right. My
suggestion is . . . Eggs Ballybeg; in other words scrambled and served on
lightly toasted caraway-seed bread. Followed—for those so inclined—by
one magnificent Wild Woodbine. Everybody happy?

Chris Excellent, Margaret!

Maggie Settled.

Rose has taken off her shoe and is examining it carefully

Agnes We'll go and pick some more bilberries next Sunday, Rosie.

Rose All right.

Agnes Remember the cans you had? You had your own two cans—
remember? Did you take them with you?

Rose Where to, Aggie?

Agnes Into the town . . . wherever you went . . .

Rose I hid them at the quarry behind a stone wall. They're safe there. I'll go
back and pick them up later this evening. Does anybody know where my
overall is?

Maggie It's lying across your bed. And you'd need to bring some turf in,
Rosie.

Rose I'll change first, Maggie.

Maggie Be quick about it.

Chris How many pieces of toast do you want?

Maggie All that loaf. And go easy on the butter—that's all we have. Now.
Parsley. And just a whiff of basil. I don't want you to be too optimistic,
girls, but you should know I feel very creative this evening.

Rose moves towards the bedroom door

Kate I want to know where you have been, Rose.

Rose stops. Pause

You have been gone for the entire afternoon. I want you to tell me where
   you've been.
Agnes Later, Kate; after——
Kate Where have you been for the past three hours?
Rose (*inaudible*) Lough Anna.
Kate I didn't hear what you said, Rose.
Rose Lough Anna.
Chris Kate, just leave——
Kate You walked from the quarry to Lough Anna?
Rose Yes.
Kate Did you meet somebody there?
Rose Yes.
Kate Had you arranged to meet somebody there?
Rose I had arranged to meet Danny Bradley there, Kate. He brought me
   out in his father's blue boat. (*To Maggie*) I don't want anything to eat,
   Maggie. I brought a bottle of milk and a packet of chocolate biscuits with
   me and we had a picnic on the lake. (*To Agnes*) Then the two of us went
   up through the back hills. He showed me what was left of the Lughnasa
   fires. A few of them are still burning away up there. (*To Kate*) We passed
   young Sweeney's house—you know, the boy who got burned, the boy you
   said was dying. Well, he's on the mend, Danny says. His legs will be
   scarred but he'll be all right. (*To all*) It's a very peaceful place up there.
   There was nobody there but Danny and me. (*To Agnes*) He calls me his
   Rosebud, Aggie. I told you that before, didn't I? (*To all*) Then he walked
   me down as far as the workhouse gate and I came on home by myself. (*To
   Kate*) And that's all I'm going to tell you. (*To all*) That's all any of you are
   going to hear.

She exits, her shoes in one hand, the poppy in the other. Michael enters

Kate What has happened to this house? Mother of God, will we ever be able
   to lift our heads ever again . . . ?

Pause

Michael The following night Vera McLaughlin arrived and explained to
   Agnes and Rose why she couldn't buy their hand-knitted gloves any
   more. Most of her home knitters were already working in the new factory
   and she advised Agnes and Rose to apply immediately. The Industrial
   Revolution had finally caught up with Ballybeg.
     They didn't apply, even though they had no other means of making a
   living, and they never discussed their situation with their sisters. Perhaps
   Agnes made the decision for both of them because she knew Rose
   wouldn't have got work there anyway. Or perhaps, as Kate believed,
   because Agnes was too notionate to work in a factory. Or perhaps the two
   of them just wanted . . . away.
     Anyway, on my first day back at school, when we came into the kitchen
   for breakfast, there was a note propped up against the milk jug: "We are
   gone for good. This is best for all. Do not try to find us." It was written in
   Agnes's resolute hand.

Of course they did try to find them. So did the police. So did our
neighbours who had a huge network of relatives all over England and
America. But they had vanished without trace. And by the time I tracked
them down—twenty-five years later, in London—Agnes was dead and
Rose was dying in a hospice for the destitute in Southwark.

The scraps of information I gathered about their lives during those
missing years were too sparse to be coherent. They had moved about a
lot. They had worked as cleaning women in public toilets, in factories, in
the Underground. Then, when Rose could no longer get work, Agnes
tried to support them both—but couldn't. From then on, I gathered, they
gave up. They took to drink; slept in parks, in doorways, on the Thames
Embankment. Then Agnes died of exposure. And two days after I found
Rose in that grim hospice—she didn't recognize me, of course—she died
in her sleep.

Father Jack's health improved quickly and he soon recovered his full
vocabulary and all his old bounce and vigour. But he didn't say Mass that
following Monday. In fact he never said Mass again. And the neighbours
stopped enquiring about him. And his name never again appeared in the
Donegal Enquirer. And of course there was never a civic reception with
bands and flags and speeches.

But he never lost his determination to return to Uganda and he still
talked passionately about his life with the lepers there. And each new
anecdote contained more revelations. And each new revelation startled—
shocked—stunned poor Aunt Kate. Until finally she hit on a phrase that
appeased her: "his own distinctive spiritual search". "Leaping around a
fire and offering a little hen to Uka or Ito or whoever is not religion as I
was taught it and indeed know it," she would say with a defiant toss of her
head. "But then Jack must make his own distinctive search." And when
he died suddenly of a heart attack—within a year of his homecoming, on
the very eve of the following Lá Lughnasa—my mother and Maggie
mourned him sorely. But for months Kate was inconsolable.

My father sailed for Spain that Saturday. The last I saw of him was
dancing down the lane in imitation of Fred Astaire, swinging his walking
stick, Uncle Jack's ceremonial tricorn at a jaunty angle over his left eye.
When he got to the main road he stopped and turned and with both hands
blew a dozen theatrical kisses back to Mother and me.

He was wounded in Barcelona—he fell off his motor-bike—so that for
the rest of his life he walked with a limp. The limp wasn't disabling but it
put an end to his dancing days; and that really distressed him. Even the
role of maimed veteran, which he loved, could never compensate for that.

He still visited us occasionally, perhaps once a year. Each time he was
on the brink of a new career. And each time he proposed to Mother and
promised me a new bike. Then the war came in 1939; his visits became
more infrequent; and finally he stopped coming altogether.

Sometime in the mid-fifties I got a letter from a tiny village in the south
of Wales; a curt note from a young man of my own age and also called
Michael Evans. He had found my name and address among the belong-
ings of his father, Gerry Evans. He introduced himself as my half-brother

and he wanted me to know that Gerry Evans, the father we shared, had died peacefully in the family home the previous week. Throughout his final illness he was nursed by his wife and his three grown children who all lived and worked in the village.

My mother never knew of that letter. I decided to tell her—decided not to—vacillated for years as my father would have done; and eventually, rightly or wrongly, kept the information to myself.

Maggie, Chris, Kate and Agnes now resume their tasks

Chris Well, at least that's good news.
Maggie What's that?
Chris That the young Sweeney boy from the back hills is going to live.
Maggie Good news indeed.

Chris goes to the door

Chris (*calling*) Michael! Where are you? We need some turf brought in! (*She now goes outside*)

Michael exits

(*Calling up to Gerry*) Are you still up there?
Gerry (*off*) Don't stand there. I might fall on top of you.
Chris Have you any idea what you're doing?
Gerry (*off*) Come on up here to me.
Chris I'm sure I will.
Gerry (*off*) We never made love on top of a sycamore tree.

She looks quickly around; did her sisters hear that?

Chris If you fall and break your neck it'll be too good for you. (*She goes inside*) Nobody can vanish quicker than that Michael fellow when you need him.
Maggie (*to Agnes*) I had a brilliant idea when I woke up this morning, Aggie. I thought to myself: what is it that Ballybeg badly needs and that Ballybeg hasn't got?
Agnes A riddle. Give up.
Maggie A dressmaker! So why doesn't Agnes Mundy who has such clever hands, why doesn't she dressmake?
Agnes Clever hands!

Maggie looks around for her cigarettes

Maggie She'd get a pile of work. They'd come to her from far and wide. She'd make a fortune.
Agnes Some fortune in Ballybeg.
Maggie And not only would the work be interesting but she wouldn't be ruining her eyes staring at grey wool eight hours a day. Did you notice how Rosie squints at things now? It's the job for you, Aggie; I'm telling you. Ah, holy God, girls, don't tell me I'm out of fags! How could that have happened?

Chris goes to the mantelpiece and produces a single cigarette

Chrissie, you are one genius. Look, Kate. (*She scowls*) Misery. (*She lights the cigarette*) Happiness! Want a drag?

Kate What's keeping those wonderful Eggs Ballybeg?

Maggie If I had to choose between one Wild Woodbine and a man of—say—fifty-two—widower—plump, what would I do, Kate? I'd take fatso, wouldn't I? God, I really am getting desperate.

Jack enters through the garden

Maybe I should go to Ryanga with you, Jack.

Jack I know you won't but I know you'd love it.

Maggie Could you guarantee a man for each of us?

Jack I couldn't promise four men but I should be able to get one husband for all of you.

Maggie Would we settle for that?

Chris One between the four of us?

Jack That's our system and it works very well. One of you would be his principal wife and live with him in his largest hut——

Maggie That'd be you, Kate.

Kate Stop that, Maggie!

Jack And the other three of you he'd keep in his enclosure. It would be like living on the same small farm.

Maggie Snug enough, girls, isn't it? (*To Jack*) And what would be—what sort of duties would we have?

Jack Cooking, sewing, helping with the crops, washing—the usual housekeeping tasks.

Maggie Sure that's what we do anyway.

Jack And looking after his children.

Maggie That he'd have by Kate.

Kate Maggie!

Jack By all four of you! And what's so efficient about that system is that the husband and his wives and his children make up a small commune where everybody helps everybody else and cares for them. I'm completely in favour of it.

Kate It may be efficient and you may be in favour of it, Jack, but I don't think it's what Pope Pius XI considers to be the holy sacrament of matrimony. And it might be better for you if you paid just a bit more attention to our Holy Father and a bit less to the Great Goddess . . . Iggie.

Music of "Anything Goes" very softly on the radio

Chris Listen.

Maggie And they have hens there, too, Jack?

Jack We're overrun with hens.

Maggie Don't dismiss it, girls. It has its points. Would you be game, Kate?

Kate Would you give my head peace, Maggie.

Chris Gerry has it going!

Maggie Tell me this, Jack: what's the Swahili for "tchook-tchook-tchook-tchook"?

Jack You'd love the climate, too, Kate.

Kate I'm not listening to a word you're saying.

Gerry runs on

Gerry Well? Any good?
Chris Listen.
Gerry Aha. Leave it to the expert.
Jack I have something for you, Gerry.
Gerry What's that?
Jack The plumed hat—the ceremonial hat—remember? We agreed to swap. With you in a second.

Jack goes to his bedroom

Maggie Good work, Gerry.
Gerry Thought it might be the aerial. That's the end of your troubles. (*He listens. He sings a line of the song*) Dance with me, Agnes.
Agnes Have a bit of sense, Gerry Evans.
Gerry Dance with me. Please. Come on.
Maggie Dance with him, Aggie.
Gerry (*singing*) "In olden times a glimpse of stocking
                    Was looked on as something shocking—"
(*Speaking*) Give me a hand.
Maggie Go on, Aggie.
Agnes Who wants to dance at this time of—

Gerry pulls her to her feet and takes her in his arms

Gerry   "... anything goes.
  (*singing*)   Good authors, too, who once knew better words
                    Now only use four-letter words
                    Writing prose,
                    Anything goes ..."

Bring up the sound. With style and with easy elegance they dance once around the kitchen and then out to the garden—Gerry singing the words directly to her face

                    If driving cars you like,
                    If low bars you like,
                    If old hymns you like,
                    If bare limbs you like,
                    If Mae West you like,
                    Or me undressed you like,
                    Why, nobody will oppose.
                    When ev'ry night, the set that's smart is
                       intruding in nudist parties in
                    Studios,
                    Anything goes ..."

They are now in the far corner of the garden

  (*Speaking*) You're a great dancer, Aggie.
Agnes No, I'm not.
Gerry You're a superb dancer.

Agnes No, I'm not.
Gerry You should be a professional dancer.
Agnes Too late for that.
Gerry You could teach dancing in Ballybeg.
Agnes That's all they need.
Gerry Maybe it is!

He bends down and kisses her on the forehead. All this is seen—but not heard—by Chris at the kitchen window. Immediately after this kiss Gerry bursts into song again, turns Agnes four or five times very rapidly and dances her back to the kitchen

There you are. Safe and sound.
Maggie I wish to God I could dance like you, Aggie.
Agnes I haven't a breath.
Gerry Doesn't she dance elegantly?
Maggie Always did, our Aggie.
Gerry Unbelievable. Now, Chrissie—you and I.
Chris (*sharply*) Not now. I wonder where Michael's got to?
Gerry Come on, Chrissie. Once round the floor.
Chris Not now, I said. Are you thick?
Maggie I'll dance with you, Gerry! (*She kicks her wellingtons off*) Do you want to see real class?
Gerry Certainly do, Maggie.
Maggie Stand back there, girls. Shirley Temple needs a lot of space.
Gerry Wow-wow-wow-wow!
Maggie Hold me close, Gerry. The old legs aren't too reliable.

She and Gerry sing and dance

Gerry }
Maggie } "In olden times a glimpse of stocking
          Was looked on as something shocking
          But now   —"

Chris suddenly turns the radio off

Chris Sick of that damned thing.
Gerry What happened?
Maggie What are you at there, Chrissie?
Chris We're only wasting the battery and we won't get a new one until the weekend.
Maggie It wasn't to be, Gerry. But there'll be another day.
Gerry That's a promise, Maggie. (*He goes to Chris at the radio*) Not a bad little set, that.
Kate Peace, thanks be to God! D'you know what that thing has done? Killed all Christian conversation in this country.
Chris (*to Agnes, icily*) Vera McLaughlin's calling here tomorrow. She wants to talk to you and Rose.
Agnes What about?
Kate (*quickly*) I didn't tell you, did I?—her daughter's got engaged!
Maggie Which of them?

Kate "The harvest dance is going to be just supreme this year, Miss
Mundy"—that wee brat!
Maggie Sophia. Is she not still at school?
Kate Left last year. She's fifteen. And the lucky man is sixteen.
Maggie Holy God. We may pack it in, girls.
Kate It's indecent, I'm telling you. Fifteen and sixteen! Don't tell me that's
not totally improper. It's the poor mother I feel sorry for.
Agnes What does she want to talk to us about?
Chris (*relenting*) Something about wool. Didn't sound important. She
probably won't call at all.

Chris turns the radio on again. No sound

(*To Maggie*) Go ahead and dance, you two.
Maggie Artistes like Margaret Mundy can't perform on demand, Chrissie.
We need to be in touch with other forces first, don't we, Gerry?
Gerry Absolutely. Why is there no sound?
Kate Maggie, are we never going to eat?
Maggie Indeed we are—outside in the garden! Eggs Ballybeg *al fresco*.
Lughnasa's almost over, girls. There aren't going to be many warm
evenings left.
Kate Good idea, Maggie.
Agnes I'll get the cups and plates.
Gerry (*with Chris at the radio*) Are you all right?
Chris It's not gone again, is it?
Gerry Have I done something wrong?
Chris I switched it on again—that's all I did.
Maggie Take out those chairs, Gerry.
Gerry What about the table?
Maggie We'll just spread a cloth on the ground. (*She goes out with the cloth
which she spreads in the middle of the garden*)

Gerry kisses Chris lightly on the back of the neck

Gerry At least we know it's not the aerial.
Chris According to you.
Gerry And if it's not the aerial the next thing to check is the ignition.
Chris Ignition! Listen to that bluffer!
Gerry Bluffer? (*To Agnes as she passes*) Did you hear what she called me?
That's unfair, Agnes, isn't it?

Agnes smiles and shrugs

Let's take the back off and see what's what.

Rose enters the garden from the back of the house

*At first nobody notices her. She is dressed as in Act I. In her right hand she
holds the dead rooster by the feet. Its feathers are ruffled and it is stained with
blood. Rose is calm, almost matter-of-fact. Agnes sees her first and goes to
her, Chris and Gerry join the others in the garden*

Agnes Rosie, what is it, Rosie?

Rose My rooster's dead.
Agnes Oh Rosie . . .
Rose (*holding the dead bird up*) Look at him. He's dead.
Agnes What happened to him?
Rose The fox must have got him.
Agnes Oh, poor Rosie . . .
Rose Maggie warned me the fox was about again. (*To all*) That's the end of my pet rooster. The fox must have got him. You were right, Maggie. (*She places it carefully on the tablecloth in the middle of the garden*)
Maggie Did he get at the hens?
Rose I don't think so.
Maggie Was the door left open?
Rose They're all right. They're safe.
Maggie That itself.
Agnes We'll get another white rooster for you, Rosie.
Rose Doesn't matter.
Maggie And I'll put manners on him early on.
Rose I don't want another.
Maggie (*quick hug*) Poor old Rosie. (*As she moves away*) We can hardly expect him to lay for us now . . .
Chris Where's that Michael fellow got to? Michael! He hears me rightly, you know. I'm sure he's jouking about out there somewhere, watching us. Michael!

Rose sits on the garden seat

Maggie All right, girls, what's missing? Knives, forks, plates——

Jack comes through the kitchen

(*Seeing Jack*) Jesus, Mary and Joseph!

Jack is wearing a very soiled, very crumpled white uniform—a version of the uniform we saw him in at the very beginning of the play. One of the epaulettes is hanging by a thread and the gold buttons are tarnished. The uniform is so large that it looks as if it were made for a much larger man: his hands are lost in the sleeves and the trousers trail on the ground. On his head he wears a tricorn, ceremonial hat; once white like the uniform but now grubby, the plumage broken and tatty. He carries himself in military style, his army cane under his arm

Jack Gerry, my friend, where are you?
Gerry Out here, Jack.
Jack There you are. (*To all*) I put on my ceremonial clothes for the formal exchange. There was a time when it fitted me—believe it or not. Wonderful uniform, isn't it?
Gerry Unbelievable. I could do with that for Spain.
Jack It was my uniform when I was chaplain to the British army during the Great War.
Kate We know only too well what it is, Jack.

Jack Isn't it splendid? Well, it was splendid. Needs a bit of a clean up. Okawa's always dressing up in it. I really must give it to him to keep.
Kate It's not at all suitable for this climate, Jack.
Jack You're right, Kate. Just for the ceremony—then I'll change back. Now, if I were at home, what we do when we swap or barter is this. I place my possession on the ground . . .

He and Gerry enact this ritual

Go ahead. (*Of hat*) Put it on the grass—anywhere—just at your feet. Now take three steps away from it—yes?—a symbolic distancing of yourself from what you once possessed. Good. Now turn round once—like this— yes, a complete circle—and that's the formal rejection of what you once had—you no longer lay claim to it. Now I cross over to where you stand—right? And you come over to the position I have left. So. Excellent. The exchange is now formally and irrevocably complete. This is my straw hat. And this is your tricorn hat. Put it on. Splendid! And it suits you! Doesn't it suit him?
Chris His head's too big.
Gerry (*adjusting the hat*) What about that? (*To Agnes*) Is that better, Agnes?
Agnes You're lovely.

Gerry does a Charlie Chaplin walk across the garden, his feet spread, his cane twirling. As he does he sings

Gerry   "In olden days a glimpse of stocking
                    Was looked on as something shocking . . ."
Jack (*adjusting his hat*) And what about this? Or like this? Or further back on my head?
Maggie Would you look at them! Strutting about like a pair of peacocks! Now—teatime!
Agnes I'll make the tea.
Maggie You can start again tomorrow. Let me finish off Lughnasa. Chrissie, put on Marconi.
Chris I think it's broken again.
Agnes Gerry fixed it. Didn't you?
Gerry Then Chrissie got at it again.
Chris Possessed that thing, if you ask me.
Kate I wish you wouldn't use words like that, Christina. There's still great heat in that sun.
Maggie Great harvest weather.
Kate I love September.
Maggie (*not moving*) Cooking time, girls.
Kate Wait a while, Maggie. Enjoy the bit of heat that's left.

Agnes moves beside Rose

Agnes Next Sunday, then. Is that all right?
Rose What's next Sunday?
Agnes We'll get some more bilberries.
Rose Yes. Yes. Whatever you say, Aggie.

Gerry examines the kites

Gerry Not bad for a kid of seven. Very neatly made.
Kate Look at the artwork.
Gerry Wow-wow-wow-wow! That is unbelievable!
Kate I keep telling his mother—she has a very talented son.
Chris So there, Mr Evans.
Gerry Have you all seen these?
Maggie I hate them.
Gerry I think they're just wonderful. Look, Jack.

For the first time we all see the images. On each kite is painted a crude, cruel, grinning face, primitively drawn, garishly painted

I'll tell you something: this boy isn't going to end up selling gramophones.
Chris Michael! He always vanishes when there's work to be done.
Maggie I've a riddle for you. Why is a gramophone like a parrot?
Kate Maggie!
Maggie Because it . . . because it always . . . because a parrot . . . God, I've forgotten! (*She moves into the kitchen*)

Michael enters

The characters are now in positions similar to their positions at the beginning of the play—with some changes: Agnes and Gerry are on the garden seat. Jack stands stiffly to attention at Agnes's elbow. One kite, facing boldly out front, stands between Gerry and Agnes; the other between Agnes and Jack. Rose is UL. *Maggie is at the kitchen window. Kate is* DR. *Chris is at the front door. During Michael's speech Kate cries quietly. As Michael begins to speak the stage is lit in a very soft, golden light so that the tableau we see is almost, but not quite, in a haze*

Michael As I said, Father Jack was dead within twelve months. And with him and Agnes and Rose all gone, the heart seemed to go out of the house.
     Maggie took on the tasks Rose and Agnes had done and pretended to believe that nothing had changed. My mother spent the rest of her life in the knitting factory—and hated every day of it. And after a few years doing nothing Kate got the job of tutoring the young family of Austin Morgan of the Arcade. But much of the spirit and fun had gone out of their lives; and when my turn came to go away, in the selfish way of young men I was happy to escape.

Now fade in very softly, just audible, the music—"It is Time to Say Goodnight" (not from the radio speaker). And as Michael continues everybody sways very slightly from side to side—even the grinning kites. The movement is so minimal that we cannot be quite certain if it is happening or if we imagine it

     And so, when I cast my mind back to that summer of 1936, different kinds of memories offer themselves to me.
     But there is one memory of that Lughnasa time that visits me most often; and what fascinates me about that memory is that it owes nothing

to fact. In that memory atmosphere is more real than incident and everything is simultaneously actual and illusory. In that memory, too, the air is nostalgic with the music of the thirties. It drifts in from somewhere far away—a mirage of sound—a dream music that is both heard and imagined; that seems to be both itself and its own echo; a sound so alluring and so mesmeric that the afternoon is bewitched, maybe haunted, by it. And what is so strange about that memory is that everybody seems to be floating on those sweet sounds, moving rhythmically, langourously, in complete isolation; responding more to the mood of the music than to its beat. When I remember it, I think of it as dancing. Dancing with eyes half closed because to open them would break the spell. Dancing as if language had surrendered to movement—as if this ritual, this wordless ceremony, was now the way to speak, to whisper private and sacred things, to be in touch with some otherness. Dancing as if the very heart of life and all its hopes might be found in those assuaging notes and those hushed rhythms and in those silent and hypnotic movements. Dancing as if language no longer existed because words were no longer necessary . . .

Slowly bring up the music. Slowly bring down the Lights

CURTAIN

FURNITURE AND PROPERTY LIST

ACT I

On stage: **KITCHEN**
Large iron range. *On it:* kettle, saucepan. *Beside it:* large turf box, pair of tongs. *On mantelpiece:* flowers
Small table. *On it:* oil lamp, thirties-style radio
Table. *On it:* iron, pile of ironing including a surplice, skirt and handkerchief
Chairs. *Over one:* Kate's cardigan
Dresser. *On shelves:* plates, saucers, etc., pair of steel knitting needles, flour-jar. *In drawer:* cutlery. *In cupboard:* wool, tablecloth
Tiny mirror on wall
Buckets of water by back door
Bucket of hen-mash by kitchen window R
Knitting (for **Agnes** and **Rose**)
Shoes (for **Maggie** and **Rose**)

GARDEN
Garden seat. *Beside it:* pieces of wood, paper, cord, etc., one almost-complete kite, basket of turf

Off stage: Shopping bags containing small, wooden spinning-top and whip, library books, bottles of cod-liver oil and quinine, various packets and jars of groceries including tea, jelly, salt, flour, butter, margarine, tapioca, sugar, etc., soap, packets of ten Woodbine cigarettes, pair of shoes, newspaper, candles, matches, apples, radio battery **(Kate)**
Roses **(Agnes)**

Personal: **Jack:** army cane
Maggie: very short cigarette butt, matches, sweet
Rose: charm and medal pinned to jumper
Gerry: walking cane (used throughout)

ACT II

Strike: Ironing and iron from kitchen table
Buckets of water by back door
Pieces of wood, paper, cord, etc., and one almost complete kite from garden

Set: **KITCHEN**
Ink bottle and some paper on table
Damp cloth
Loaf of bread on table
Single cigarette on mantelpiece

GARDEN
Two finished kites against garden seat

Off stage: Two zinc buckets of water **(Maggie)**
Armful of clothes **(Kate)**
Two small pails of blackberries **(Agnes)**
Red poppy **(Rose)**
Dead, white rooster **(Rose)**

Personal: **Jack:** army cane

LIGHTING PLOT

Property fittings required: nil

Interior and exterior setting. The same scene throughout

ACT I

To open: Spotlight on **Michael**

Cue 1	As **Michael** begins to speak *Slowly bring up lighting on tableau*	(Page 1)
Cue 2	**Michael:** ". . . I had a chance to observe him." *Cross-fade to warm summer afternoon effect*	(Page 2)

ACT II

To open: Late summer afternoon effect

Cue 3	**Michael:** "As I said." *Cross-fade to very soft, golden light on tableau*	(Page 55)
Cue 4	**Michael:** ". . . were no longer necessary . . ." *Slowly fade to Black-out*	(Page 56)

EFFECTS PLOT

ACT I

Cue 1   **Rose** turns on the radio   (Page 3)
Loud, three-second blast of "The British Grenadiers"

Cue 2   **Chris** switches on the radio   (Page 16)
Slowly bring up Irish dance music: "The Mason's Apron", from radio: barely audible at first, gradually increasing in volume; when ready cut music in mid-phrase, leaving short bursts of static from radio

Cue 3   **Chris** switches off the radio   (Page 17)
Cut static noises

Cue 4   **Gerry:** "Lucky boy."   (Page 24)
An appropriate song of the period plays softly from the radio

Cue 5   **Gerry** and **Chris** dance off   (Page 26)
Continue song for few seconds more then cut off in mid-phrase

ACT II

Cue 6   **Kate:** "...the Great Goddess ... Iggie."   (Page 49)
Music: "Anything Goes" very softly on radio

Cue 7   **Gerry** (singing): "Writing prose/Anything goes ..."   (Page 50)
Increase volume

Cue 8   **Chris** suddenly turns the radio off   (Page 51)
Cut music

Cue 9   **Michael:** "... I was happy to escape."   (Page 55)
            Fade in very softly music: "It is Time to Say Good-night"

Cue 10   **Michael:** "... were no longer necessary ..."   (Page 56)
            Slowly increase music volume

MADE AND PRINTED IN GREAT BRITAIN BY
LATIMER TREND & COMPANY LTD PLYMOUTH

MADE IN ENGLAND